IN AND FOR
THE WORLD

Bringing the Contemporary into Christian Worship

Paul B. Brown

FORTRESS PRESS   **MINNEAPOLIS**

To Bev, Chris, and Shelley.

IN AND FOR THE WORLD
Bringing the Contemporary into Christian Worship

Copyright © 1992 Augsburg Fortress. All rights reserved. Except for brief quotations in critical articles or reviews, no part of this book may be reproduced in any manner without prior written permission from the publisher. Write to: Permissions, Augsburg Fortress, 426 S. Fifth St., Box 1209, Minneapolis, MN 55440.

Scripture quotations unless otherwise noted are from the New Revised Standard Version Bible, copyright © 1989 by the Division of Christian Education of the National Council of the Churches of Christ in the United States.

Cover design and illustration: Terry Bentley

Library of Congress Cataloging-in-Publication Data

Brown, Paul B.
   In and for the world : bringing the contemporary into Christian
worship / Paul B. Brown.
     p.   cm.
   Includes bibliographical references and index.
   ISBN 0-8006-2657-5
    1. Public worship.   2. Language and languages—Religious aspects—
Christianity. 3. Church. I. Title.
BV15.B76   1992
264'.0014—dc20   92-7933
                                                      CIP

The paper used in this publication meets the minimum requirements of American National Standard for Information Sciences—Permanence of Paper for Printed Library Materials, ANSI Z329.48-1984. ∞™

Manufactured in the U.S.A.   AF 1-2657

96   95   94   93   92   1   2   3   4   5   6   7   8   9   10

Contents

Acknowledgments

Preface

Properly conceived, the liturgical heritage of the church reflects the church's mission to its contemporary culture. The church's purpose is not primarily to keep its traditions alive, but to communicate those traditions to the world it is in, bringing God's redemptive reign to bear upon human culture. As such, the church's liturgical tradition and its saving mission converge to become the body of Christ at work at every contemporaneous point of history.

In and for the World asserts that the church's worship should reflect the church's purpose. Liturgical language needs to connect with its contemporary world; otherwise, the church's worship becomes largely irrelevant to the world for which it exists. How the church speaks and what it speaks about in its liturgies will disclose that today's church exists in behalf of today's world, that it is not indifferent to contemporary realities but is engaged with them redemptively.

The purpose of this book is to explore ways the worship of today's church will reflect its engagement with the realities of its culture. The book began as a series of lectures, titled "Worldly Church, Worldly Language," given as the Bowen Lectures at Memphis Theological Seminary in the spring of 1990.

Chapter 1 centers the church's mission on the image of the church as the body of Christ. As the body of Christ, the church is in and for the world; it is not a haven or a retreat from the realities of contemporary life, however harsh, but rather is engaged with those realities in redemptive and transforming ways. At the same time the church does not submit to worldly authority. Under the reign of God, the church is countercultural; it stands over against the sin and evil of its social environment, refusing to compromise with worldly standards, values, and constructs of reality.

Since liturgy is the voice of the church in its worship, chapter 2 examines the nature and place of liturgical language. Like all language, liturgical language is not neutral or benign but powerfully creative, opening up new vistas, providing new ways of constructing reality. So what is spoken in worship matters. This chapter is also concerned with how the church's language is understood. Much liturgical speech consists of a specialized vocabulary—the terminology of Christian faith. Yet, although the church has to use the sacred speech of its faith, it also needs to put its special language into the idiom of its own time.

The next three chapters build upon the assumptions set forth in the first two. If the church's purpose is to be Christ's body in behalf of the world, and if the language of its worship is powerfully constructive, then the language of the church will communicate the purpose of the church. These chapters offer suggestions and examples for how the church's being in and for the world can be communicated through the church's liturgical speech—in its sermons, hymns, prayers, creeds, and scripture readings. Chapter 3 examines ways of using language that is concrete rather than abstract, specific rather than general, public rather than private. The language of the church's worship will reflect the church's connection with the ongoing events of its global context without compromising its biblical and theological traditions.

If the church is the body of Christ in contemporary society, its worship will be representative of the wide variety of society's people. Chapter 4 focuses on the inclusive nature of the church and its worship. The use of inclusive language in worship represents the equal status of women with men and broadens images of God beyond the masculine. The language of liturgy is also nondiscriminatory, showing a concern for persons whom society in general may exclude from social acceptability, and using terms of designation that dignify persons who are marginalized or are members of minority groups.

Chapter 5 extends the focus of Christian worship outward to cover the globe. The victories and defeats, joys and griefs, and issues and interests of the whole world are also those of the local parish. The sermons, prayers, hymns, and creeds of a particular people at worship name the realities of people everywhere because the church exists in their behalf. The global nature of Christ's church can be affirmed by including linguistically worship traditions that come from widely varying cultures. The use of multinational liturgical resources enables a church in one nation to enrich and broaden its theological perspective by participating in the faith language of another.

The Bibliography offers a selection of recent liturgical resources that are pertinent to the major areas of concern in the book. Annotations are included for sections on Global and Ecumenical Resources, Contemporary Prayers, Composing Corporate Prayers, Hymnbooks, and Religious Periodicals, directed to pastors, worship committees, and lay leaders who may wish to consult resources beyond the ones mentioned in the book.

A number of the direct citations that appear in the text are in male-exclusive language. They have been included because they contribute substantially to the discussion at hand, although they will be jarring to gender-sensitive readers. The quotations are given in their original version or translation, without the use of brackets or other means of rendering them gender-inclusive, as such efforts generally call attention to the language more than minimize it. I trust that as they read the citations, readers mentally will make inclusive substitutions.

I am indebted to a number of persons and institutions who helped me complete this project. The Association of Theological Schools granted me a stipend from the Lilly Foundation, and Memphis Theological Seminary provided me a three-month sabbatical leave. Wesley Theological Seminary in Washington, D.C., graciously made available living quarters and full use of their study resources during my leave. Resources too numerous to mention were provided by worshiping communities and their leaders in the Washington, D.C., area. Constructive critiques of my manuscript were contributed by colleagues Mary Lin Hudson, Robert Brawley, and Hubert Morrow, by James M. Schellman, Associate Executive Secretary of the International Commission on English in the Liturgy, and by my friends, pastors James Knight and Roy Hall. Students, as they became familiar with my project, made helpful comments and steered me toward resources.

Deeper appreciation than these lines can show goes to my wife, Beverly, and children, Shelley and Chris, for their willingness to assume added family responsibilities during my sabbatical leave, and to my father, Paul F., for his support and continued interest in my work.

1

Bringing the Contemporary into Worship

On Saturday night, Christmas Eve 1988, my daughter Shelley and I decided to attend a midnight service. We selected a church in midtown Memphis and joined about five hundred worshipers in a service of carols, prayers, and Eucharist.

For us Memphians, the week had been a devastating one. On the previous Wednesday, Pan Am Flight 103, having departed London for New York, had exploded in mid-air and plunged down upon the quiet Scottish village of Lockerbie. All 259 passengers, many on their way home for Christmas, were killed, along with eleven villagers on the ground. Investigators were saying that a terrorist bomb likely caused the explosion. Then on Friday, two days before Christmas, a tanker truck loaded with propane gas careened out of control on an exit ramp off Interstate 240 in midtown Memphis, slammed into a bridge abutment, and exploded in a massive fireball. Five people were killed in their cars on the highway. Three others in homes nearby died from the explosion, including Shalanda Toles, age 10, when the truck's rear axles catapulted into the air and crashed down into the room where she was playing near the family Christmas tree.

The media were giving saturation coverage to these back-to-back tragedies; throughout Memphis questions were being asked, lives mourned, shock expressed. Many of us attending the Christmas Eve service that Saturday night in one way or another had been trying to sort through our emotions and reactions to those disasters, to the suffering, the deaths, the innocent victims, the terrorism. Yet, at that service, neither of the two tragedies was ever alluded to, much less explicitly mentioned—even though the truck explosion had occurred only thirty-six hours earlier and not more than five blocks away.

The liturgy was beautiful, filled with the festive sounds, colors, and words appropriate to Christmastime. Yet, when the liturgy was over I left the church feeling that something had not been entirely right about it. How strange for all of us recently to have been so close to tragedy, for it to be a part of our collective awareness, yet not to have spoken it, not to have named before God what was there all around and inside us. As I drove home that Christmas Eve night, it occurred to me that the liturgy, as beautiful as it was, could have been done on almost any other Christmas Eve: last year, the year before, ten years ago.

Granted, Christian worship has important dimensions other than its contemporary relevance. Worship is a people's celebrative response before their God, it is the taking of eucharistic bread and wine, it is hearing the gospel read and proclaimed, it is both the personal apprehension of the presence of God and the experience of community in Christ. Worship is all of this and more. Still, every event of worship occurs in some historical context. Worship has a time and a place; it is done somewhere at some time. The circumstances of any particular time and place impinge upon and affect the lives of all the people who gather to say the prayers, sing the hymns, and take the bread and wine. But, should not the special circumstances of a particular time and place that people bring with them to worship in some way be named before God? If not, if current historical realities are omitted from the language of a congregation's liturgy, then many persons experience that the church's worship is somehow indifferent to the church's historical context, that a part of their existence has been left untouched by the worship event.

Sometimes the expression "out of touch" is used to describe a person, as in "she seems to be out of touch with what's going on in her family," in other words, not being alert or sensitive to ongoing events or being disengaged from some dimension of reality. If our liturgies do not speak of what is immediate to our historical experience, then we might ask if such worship is really in touch with that experience. If the church's liturgical language, especially its preaching and prayers, is indirect and nonspecific, or if it is a language so closely attached to its liturgical tradition that it does not speak to contemporary conditions, then it may also be remote from human experience, from what we call "real life," from the very world the church is meant to serve.

2

The Christmas Eve episode is recounted as a striking example of when the language of the liturgy falls short of lifting up before God the contemporary historical realities in which it is being spoken. To be sure, few worship services take place in the midst of such dramatic and wrenching occurrences as this one (thank God!). Every service of worship needs to be contextual, that is, it needs to take account of its historical context that includes needs, failures, accomplishments, conflicts, successes, injustices, and blessings—the stuff of life and experience. Although not all (perhaps, not even many) components of any particular historical context can possibly be addressed in any single worship event, nonetheless a service of Christian worship needs to demonstrate that it is in touch with the historical circumstances of its time through the language of its liturgy: by what it talks about, speaks in behalf of, warns against, prays over, reflects upon.

In the introduction to her collection of contemporary prayers, Vienna Cobb Anderson says that "the tragedy of liturgy today is that we have made the language of worship so abstract that it is nearly impossible to sense the joy and blessing of life in an earthy and real way. . . . Week after week, many of us have been burdened by the weight of a language that neither names our dreams, struggles, or sorrows, nor offers us the consolation of feeling named or affirmed as full members of the Body of Christ." The consequence often is that persons leave the church and its worship, finding that "the language of worship seems so foreign to the longings, doubts, and fears of their hearts . . . [or] assuming that whatever happens inside is archaic and irrelevant to their own life experiences."[1]

The language Christians use in their worship—how they speak and what they speak about—represents the most obvious and direct way the church's worship connects with the world the church is in. Through the language of its preaching, its hymnody, its thanksgivings, its confessions, and its corporate intercessory prayers, the contemporary church is able to claim its relevance to the events of its time. To one degree or another, or to whatever degree possible, the language of Christian liturgies will reflect the contemporary historical contexts in which it is being spoken.

1. Vienna Cobb Anderson, *Prayers of Our Hearts in Word and Action* (New York: Crossroad, 1991) xi. The prayers in her book represent an effort to address the situation she describes by providing—as a supplement to her own denominational prayerbook—prayers that address a wide-ranging assortment of modern needs and conditions.

The Church as the Body of Christ

A splendid multiplicity of metaphors and images for the church are sprinkled throughout the New Testament, such as a holy nation (1 Pet. 2:9), the people of God (Rom. 9:25), the new creation (2 Cor. 5:17), the household of God (1 Pet. 4:17), and the bride of Christ (2 Cor. 11:1).[2] Among Paul's (and deutero-Pauline) epistles, the church as the body of Christ figures predominantly (Rom. 7:4; 12:4-8; 1 Cor. 10:16,17; 11:27, 29; 12:12-27; cf. Col. 1:18, 24; 3:15; Eph. 2:16; 4:4)[3] and provides us a way for understanding how the church is related with the world in which it exists.

The apostle nowhere explains or develops his metaphor for the church, and the various nuances he gives to the word *body* in his writings create enormous difficulties for interpreters trying to build a systematic, coherent Pauline ecclesiology. For example, it is not always clear whether Paul is using the term literally for Jesus or figuratively for the church. Yet, that the image is central to Paul's ecclesiology is not in doubt. Paul's use of it without explanation may even show that he has already adopted the metaphor himself and that it is familiar enough to his readers to warrant no further development.[4] Paul connects it with both baptism ("for by one Spirit we were all baptized into one body" [1 Cor. 12:13]) and the communal meal ("because there is one bread, we who are many are one body, for we all partake of the one bread" [1 Cor. 10:17]). Indeed, in Paul's thinking the relationship between the church as body and Christ as body is so close that a fracturing of the one equals a fracturing of the other: "Each of you says, 'I belong to Paul,' or 'I belong to Apollos,' or 'I belong to Christ.' Has Christ been divided?" (1 Cor. 1:12,13a).

Without trying to reconcile the nuances of meaning and the interpretive questions that surround Paul's metaphor of the church as Christ's body, several conclusions may be drawn from the image. First, through the church as the body of Christ the believer is incorporated into the saving work of the crucified and risen Lord. Paul understands

2. Paul S. Minear (*Images of the Church in the New Testament* [Philadelphia: Westminster Press, 1960]) finds ninety-six images or "analogies" for the church in the New Testament.

3. Ernst Käsemann (*Commentary on Romans,* trans. Geoffrey W. Bromiley [Grand Rapids, Mich.: Wm. B. Eerdmans, 1980], 335) says the motif "is characteristic for [Paul's] ecclesiology."

4. So Käsemann, *Commentary on Romans,* 338.

membership in the body of Christ to be "a participation in the eschatological saving event which has begun through Christ."[5] Through baptism, the believer joins with a community of believers who are "in Christ," that is, those who have experienced the saving activity of God in Christ.

Second, the church as Christ's body represents for Paul the church's divine origin and the transcendent authority of Christ over it. Although the community is not in a literal sense Christ's body (the church is not the body of deity), it is his body in the sense of being "the earthly sphere of power" of the exalted Christ.[6] For this reason, the apostle is able to appeal to the church's mystical relationship with Christ as an answer even to ethical disputes and questions of church polity. For example, Rudolf Bultmann notes that Paul uses "the body of Christ" in 1 Corinthians 12 not merely to show that believers comprise an organic, unified community. "His main thought is, rather, that the members are equal because they belong to Christ, and therefore their differences are unimportant (v. 12f.). It is not the members that constitute the body but Christ (Rom. 12:5 implies the same). Christ is there, not through and in the members, but before they are there and above them."[7]

Third, the church as Christ's body helps to define for Paul the church's purpose, to determine its work. It is not incidental that Paul's use of the image usually occurs when he is describing what Christian believers do or how they act (or ought to act).[8] For example, in 1 Corinthians 12, as in Romans 12, the apostle interprets the various gifts given to the members of the community as services or contributions to the welfare of each other and to the church as a whole. Gifts of preaching or healing or doing miracles or leading or even speaking in tongues—these are all acts of service meant to benefit each other, to serve each other. In short, because the church is the body of Christ, how it acts is determined by how Christ acts; the life of the church is determined by the Christ event.[9]

5. Werner Georg Kümmel, *The Theology of the New Testament* (Nashville: Abingdon Press, 1973), 210.

6. Käsemann, *Commentary on Romans*, 336.

7. Rudolf Bultmann, *Theology of the New Testament*, trans. Kendrick Grobel (New York: Charles Scribner's Sons, 1951), 1:310.

8. That Paul uses the term in reference to *local* congregations does not lessen its significance because, for Paul, the local church always represents the whole church (Käsemann, *Commentary on Romans*, 336).

9. Because, as Bultmann notes, in the primitive church "the proclaimer became the

This understanding of the church is similar to the one held by the writer of Luke-Acts. According to Luke, after the resurrected Jesus ascended into heaven (Acts 1:6-11), the cluster of Christian believers he left behind was formed into a community by the event of Pentecost (Acts 2): the church succeeds the earthly Jesus. As Jesus was born by the Holy Spirit (Luke 1:35), the church is born by the Holy Spirit (Acts 2). As Jesus performed the redemptive work of God in history through the Spirit (the Gospel of Luke), so the church continues the work of God in history under the power of the same Spirit (Acts of the Apostles). Indeed, when Paul is on the road to Damascus in zealous persecution of the church, he is struck down by a vision of the risen Lord, who asks him, "Saul, Saul, why are you persecuting me?" (Acts 9:4) So while the ascended Christ is seated at the right hand of God in heaven, the church continues as the eschatological community of Christ on earth.[10]

This Pauline metaphor greatly influenced Dietrich Bonhoeffer, for whom the church exists contextually at the center of history. "We should think of the church not as an institution, but as a *person*, though of course a person in a unique sense,"[11] he wrote. The empirical church was created by God to be God's historical community at work to save the world, and, as the body of Christ, "[it] is the presence of Christ in the world."[12] For Bonhoeffer, the church as Christ's body is no simple metaphor; it conveys the mystical reality of the presence of Jesus Christ in the world, the means through which human beings are able to experience the divine.

> [Jesus Christ] comes to us to-day, and is present with us in bodily form and in his word. If we would hear his call to follow, we must listen where he is to be found, that is, in the Church through the ministry of Word and Sacrament . . . If you would hear the call of Jesus you need no

---

proclaimed" (*Theology*, 1:33), it is not only the historical Jesus that is normative for the church, but the whole Christ event.

10. See Hans Conzelmann, *The Theology of St. Luke,* trans. Geoffrey Buswell (New York: Harper & Row, 1961), 206. The other three Gospel writers did not produce a second volume like Acts, yet the Jesus of Matthew's Gospel does anticipate the emergence of the church: "You are Peter, and upon this rock I will build my church" (16:18) ". . . and the Great Commission" (28:18-20).

11. Dietrich Bonhoeffer, *Act and Being,* trans. Bernard Noble (New York: Harper & Row, 1961), 185.

12. Dietrich Bonhoeffer, *The Communion of Saints,* trans. R. Gregor Smith (New York: Harper & Row, 1963), 197.

personal revelation: all you have to do is hear the sermon and receive the sacrament, that is, to hear the gospel of Christ crucified and risen. Here he is, the same Christ whom the disciples encountered, the same Christ whole and entire. Yes, here he is already, the glorified, victorious and living Lord. Only Christ himself can call us to follow him.[13]

Paul does not provide us with a full description of the historical implications of his view of the church as the body of Christ. The apostle clearly expected the imminent return of Christ and, with it, the consummation of history (for example, 1 Cor. 15:23; 1 Thess. 2:19; 3:13; 4:15; 2 Thess. 2:1, 8-9). Yet, because the church has continued to exist within history for these nearly two millennia, we will need to draw historical implications from Paul's image. If today's church is the body of Christ, then in what way is the church in relation to its historical context?

The Church and the World

As the body of Jesus Christ, the church is in and among, not above or beyond, the ongoing events taking place in the historical present. Jesus was God-in-the-world, living, working, preaching, dying—all in the world. A history that was not worthy of him still became the history that was his own. It is often noted that Jesus' ministry took place outside the religious institutions of his day, primarily because those institutions had become fixed systems, closed off from and indifferent to their own earthly, historical context. So Jesus' advent was not into some world-within-a-world, such as an established in-group, but rather, it was to the whole world of human experience: being born and making a living and paying taxes and eating and drinking—all of life, brought under the reign of God. Because death also is a part of earthly experience, Jesus died so that his death, along with the injustice and suffering and dirty politics that went along with it, would be placed under the reign of God. Jesus was in the world; as the hymn depicts it, "joy of heaven to earth come down."

The Church in History

Just so, the Christian church is in the world. As the body of Christ, it remains inseparably engaged with time and geography. We speak

13. Dietrich Bonhoeffer, *The Cost of Discipleship,* trans. R. H. Fuller, rev. ed. (New York: Macmillan Company, 1959), 201-2.

of people who "live in their own little worlds": lovers, maybe, whose interest in life is limited to their own romance, or professional people whose "work is their life." But the church as the body of Christ has no such world-within-the-world. The church, as Robert Hovda says, is not "a retreat from life, an island protecting us from the mainland."[14] Earthly and worldly, the church has nothing to hide and nowhere to hide because it seeks to expose all of life as under the reign of God. The church is in the world as yeast is in bread, as salt is in food, or as a candle is in a dark room, to recall Jesus' metaphors. The church knows its place: wide open and vulnerable, the church is *in* history.

The importance of this surely is seen in the Johannine account of Jesus' prayer just before his death: "I do not pray that you should take [my disciples] out of the world, but that you should keep them from the evil one" (John 17:15). Could it be that the Christian community of John was among the first to get notions about becoming spiritually or institutionally detached from its messy world? To be sure, the church has been accused, rightly on occasion, of what might be called "ecclesiological Docetism": the appearance of being in history without the reality. Matthew Fox tells about a woman who had worked for many years with prostitutes on the streets of Chicago. Once she was asked if she had received much support from the churches in caring for these women. "No," she replied, "none whatsoever." "What do you think of the church?" she was asked. "I see the church as a very, very old grandmother who does not see well anymore, does not hear well anymore, and does not get out much anymore."[15]

Again, sometimes we conceive of the church as a refuge or sanctuary, in the sense that through it we participate in the religious traditions and rituals that uniquely define our nature as the family of God, and that in its worship we turn aside from all else to focus our energies on the God of all life and history. But we should be careful that terms like *refuge, haven,* and *sanctuary* do not lead us to thinking of the church as a place of escape from the dreary and often painful circumstances of life in the world.[16]

14. Robert Hovda, "Amen Corner," *Worship* 58 (January 1984): 51.
15. Matthew Fox, *The Coming of the Cosmic Christ* (New York: Harper & Row, 1988), 27.
16. Church architecture can create distance between a church and its historical milieu: for example, medieval (or ersatz colonial) styles and stained-glass windows that serve as visual barriers between worshipers and world.

The church is a sanctuary in the world, not a sanctuary from the world. It is not a place of escape from this present time to some other time or from this world into some other world. Its worship is not indifferent to the events of the history in which we live, much less aloof from them. Worship is not reality-denial; it is reality-adjustment. Worship corrects our perspective: the daily affairs of all existence are gathered up and cast under the light of the sovereignty and love of God in Christ, thereby giving them their true context and meaning. When we worship, we do not take a historical leave-of-absence in order to enter some different level or realm of experience; rather, we bring into worship the historical realities of our existence and place them under the reign of God so that we can understand them for what they are. In the words of John Melloh, the worshiping people of God view the world "through gospel-colored glasses and not merely rose-tinted contact lenses."[17]

In post-exilic Judaism, some priests, while serving at the altar, would wear robes decorated with sun, moon, and stars in order to express the belief that the altar is the center of the universe and that in worship chaos becomes cosmos.[18] The church is demonstrably in history.

The Church for History

All of the creative acts of God in history, from creation to parousia, are done in behalf of God's world. John 3:16 is not merely a verse to be memorized at Bible school or a reference to be displayed at sporting events. It describes in a word the purpose of God's creative activity: the self-giving of God is in behalf of the world God loves, inexplicable as that may be.

One of the valuable contributions to come from Vatican II is the emphasis on the church as the *sacramentum mundi*, "the sacrament given to the world to serve the world."[19] The Christian church is for history; its locus is the here and now in behalf of persons, especially persons whose lives have been marginalized by injustice, powerlessness, dis-

17. John Melloh, "The Prayer of Participation," in Virgil C. Funk, ed., *Children, Liturgy, and Music* (Washington, D.C.: The Pastoral Press, 1990), 6.

18. Fred B. Craddock, *Preaching* (Nashville: Abingdon Press, 1985), 42.

19. Theodore Runyon, "World as Original Sacrament," *Worship* 54 (November 1980): 503.

ease, or poverty. It loves the world with a Godly love, it loves the world sacramentally. As Jesus entered human history to serve as God's saving presence and witness, so the church as the body of Christ continues to exist in history, still serving as God's saving presence and witness.

The church's worship, too, is for history. Sometimes we might be tempted to think of worship as being separate from ministry in society: as if we step out of our historical setting at eleven o'clock on Sunday morning, and then, when the service concludes, go back into the world to serve God. But because the church is for the world, there can be no essential separation between the worship of God and the service of God; we affirm this even with our terminology: "worship service," "A Service of Word and Sacrament." In addition, there is even a sense in which we can speak of vicarious worship, in that worshipers never worship wholly for themselves individually, but always in behalf of others as well.

1) Our liturgical **praise and thanksgivings** reflect not only how God has blessed each of us singularly but all of us collectively—in fact, they show how interconnected individual blessings are with corporate blessings. This is clearly the case in the Psalter. Psalm 103 begins personally but ends collectively: "Bless the Lord, O my soul; and all that is within me, bless God's holy name . . . Bless the Lord, O you God's angels . . . all God's hosts . . . all God's works."

2) **Confessions of sin** are not made exclusively for the worshipers' personal sins but for the sins of all. In the worship tradition of Israel, the sins of the nation and even the entire social order were a part of each person's doing and so were a part of each person's guilt. So the prophet Isaiah prayed, "I am a man of unclean lips, and I dwell in the midst of a people of unclean lips."

3) The **collection of offerings** is taken not only for the institutional needs of a particular congregation but for the congregation's larger ministries in the world as well, through its own service programs and through denominational social agencies.

4) The **proclamation of the gospel** in the liturgy is not intended to be for insiders only, but for those outside the church as well. Bonhoeffer considered the church's proclamation of the gospel as the primary means of divine influence upon the world. It is redemptive in that "it has overcome the disunions, tensions, and conflicts between the

'Christian' element and the 'secular' element . . . in the belief that the reconciliation of the world with God has been accomplished."[20]

5) Certainly the celebration of the **Eucharist** acts to incorporate every worshiper around the worldwide table of Christ: every celebration reminds communicants that "people shall come from east and west and north and south and sit at table in the kingdom of God" (Luke 13:29). A hymn by Brian Wren expresses this eucharistic unity. The hymn begins with the Eucharist being experienced by persons as individuals:

> *I* come with joy to meet *my* Lord, forgiven, loved, and free,
> in awe and wonder to recall His life laid down for *me*.

But the individuals merge with other persons to form community:

> *I* come *with Christians* far and near to find, as all are fed,
> The new *community* of love in Christ's communion bread.

> As Christ breaks bread and bids *us* share, each proud division ends.
> The love that made *us*, makes *us* one, and strangers now are friends.

And the new community then reaches out to encompass the world:

> Together met, together bound, we'll go our different ways,
> And as his people *in the world,* we'll live and speak His praise.[21]

Most eucharistic liturgies include the Agnus Dei: "O Lamb of God, who takes away the sin of the world, have mercy on us." The sacramental elements of bread and wine serve to unite worshipers as advocates for persons who are hungry throughout the world.

6) The sacrament of **Baptism** affirms that becoming a Christian is not merely an individual decision or experience. In baptism we are joined to the worldwide community of faith both on earth and in heaven, and participate in the ongoing work of God in salvation history.

7) Then, worship in behalf of the world is expressed in the liturgical **prayers of intercession.** These prayers naturally will voice the intercessions for the immediate community: one's self, family, friends, and other members of the church community; but just as naturally they

---

20. Dietrich Bonhoeffer, *Ethics,* ed. Eberhard Bethge (New York: Macmillan Company, 1962), 263.
21. *The Presbyterian Hymnal* (Louisville: Westminster/John Knox, 1990), 507. Italics added.

will reach beyond every boundary—race, culture, economics, politics, ideology, geography—to voice intercessions for sisters and brothers who, though they may not be known by the community, are known about. Any liturgy that fails to present before God intercessions in behalf of the larger community of God is incomplete if not truncated, in that it fails to demonstrate its nature to be for the world. Again, because the Psalms are ancient liturgical prayers, they can serve as examples of this larger social concern. Although some are prayed in the first person (Ps. 26: "Vindicate me, O Lord, for I have walked in my integrity"), others are pleas for cities and nations, even the cosmos (Ps. 5: "Let all who take refuge in you rejoice, let them sing for joy; and do defend them, O God, that those who love your name may exult in you"; Ps. 9: "Arise, O Lord! Let not mere humans prevail; let the nations be judged before you"; Ps. 10: "O God, lift up your hand; forget not the afflicted"; Ps. 22: "Redeem Israel, O God, out of all its troubles").

Because the church, like its Lord, is in the world and for the world, it is indissolubly linked with history. As Wesley Granberg-Michaelson concludes: "The church is called neither to a life in and for itself, nor to treat the creation chiefly as an antagonist. Rather, the community of faith is to be the vessel through which the life of Jesus Christ can take on flesh and bones today, extending God's love to the whole created world. The grace of Jesus Christ and the power of the Holy Spirit calls the church into being for the sake of the whole world's life."[22]

This means that the language of the church's liturgies will reflect the contemporary realities that comprise the historical arena in which the liturgy is done. When that language is indifferent to its historical context or is only vaguely spoken, then distance develops between the church and its place in the world. But when that language reflects both the traditional faith expressions of the people of God and the circumstances of the time and place in which it is being spoken, then the church is more clearly living out its nature to be the Lord's body.

Not the Church of History

It is important to say that, although the church is in and for the world, it is not of the world. We have already seen that in Paul's understanding,

22. Wesley Granberg-Michaelson, *A Worldly Spirituality: The Call to Redeem Life on Earth* (New York: Harper & Row, 1984), 146–47.

the church as Christ's body means that it is of God so its origin is divine, not human: "She is His new creation by water and the Word," in the words of the hymn. A subtle danger always exists: that a conviction that the church is in the world should lead to the belief that the church is also of the world. But although the church represents God's work in behalf of the world, at the same time it represents God's judgment over against the world, because the church, like its Lord, resists and rejects what is evil in history.

The redemptive message of Jesus was often a message of cultural reversal: the first will be last and the last first (Mark 10:31); the meek, not the strong, are the ones who are blessed (Matt. 5:5); the exalted will be humbled and the humble exalted (Luke 14:11). The theme continues in the early church: God chooses what is foolish in the world to shame the wise, what is weak in the world to shame the powerful, and what the world thinks is nothing to destroy what the world thinks is important (1 Cor. 1:27,28 GNB). In every age when the church makes a serious and disciplined response to the gospel, it finds itself on a collision course with popular culture. For example, in the late 1970s, when members of a basic Christian community near the capital city of El Salvador began to take up the cause of the poor, challenging the traditional church, they stirred up opposition. "These people aren't Catholics," critics would say, "they're *subversives!*"[23]

James W. Fowler points out that the countercultural nature of biblical faith occurs in a repetitive pattern in numerous biblical texts. The encounter between humans and God "begins with a *destabilizing* or *deconstruction* of the world's sign system dealing with power."[24] For example, Psalm 146 begins with "Alleluia! Praise Yahweh, my soul!" which serves to turn us away from ourselves, our culture, conventional morality—the "fleshly" or "worldly" dimension of existence, as Paul might call it. It "draws us out from self-absorption and detaches us from centers of value and power other than the Holy One."[25] This initial stage of deconstruction, though, is followed by a reconstruction, that is, a "revisioning of power, . . . an alternative way of being in

23. Pablo Galdamez, *Faith of a People* (Maryknoll, N.Y.: Orbis Books, 1986), 17. Emphasis on the original.

24. James W. Fowler, *Weaving the New Creation: Stages of Faith and the Public Church* (San Francisco: Harper San Francisco, 1991), 175. Original emphasis.

25. Fowler, *Weaving*, 175.

the world and in ecclesial community."[26] The rest of the psalm draws in sharp relief the radical power and purposes of God, who:

> gives justice to the oppressed,
> gives food to the hungry,
> sets prisoners free,
> gives sight to the blind,
> lifts up the bowed down,
> protects the stranger,
> sustains the orphan and the widow,
> loves the upright,
> frustrates the wicked.

According to the psalmist, this is what is real and right and true; this is the real world, the world reconstructed in accordance to the will of God.[27] Just so, Jesus' own person embodied the reconstruction of the world as represented by the reign of God: "You have heard it said, . . . but I say to you." As the body of Christ, the church continues as God's agent of reconstruction. One answer the El Salvadoran Christians in our story above might well give their critics is, "We are not subversive so much as we are reconstructed!"

It has to be acknowledged that altogether too often in its history the church has not been an agent of reconstruction, much less subversive. It would be difficult to overstate the times and ways the church has allowed its theology to fall under the influence of prevailing secular culture. Several contemporary examples come to mind: the "success-and-prosperity gospel,"[28] nationalistic civil religion and its counterpart, "don't-rock-the-boat" political neutrality,[29] the "warm and cozy"

---

26. Fowler, *Weaving,* 175.

27. Other texts that show the same pattern, according to Fowler, are Philippians 2:5-11 and Matthew 9:9-17, Isaiah 42 and 61, Luke 4:16-20, 1 Corinthians 12, Romans 12, and Galatians 3:28.

28. Robert Tilton's "Success-N-Life" television markets have grown to more than ninety, making it "the fastest-growing empire in Christian television" (Scott Baradell, "The Prophet of Prosperity," *Dallas Times Herald,* 24 June 1990, sec. A, p. 21).

29. In response to the United States' bombing of Iraq, the president of the Shelby Baptist Association, a union of 124 local Southern Baptist churches, said, "The whole thrust of the Bible . . . is that man has the definite right to protect himself, families have that right, and nations have that right" (*The Commercial Appeal,* 17 January 1991, sec. A, p. 10). Central North Church raised a 12-by-18-foot U.S. flag on the 100-foot mast that supports the Christian cross (*The Commercial Appeal,* 18 January 1991, sec. B, p. 4), and an "Americans United for Patriotism" rally, complete with the Millington Naval Air Station's Flying Rifle Drill team, was held at the St. Louis Catholic Church (*The Commercial Appeal,* 29 January 1991, sec. A, p. 7).

church of suburbia,[30] positive thinking and self-help groups,[31] the individualistic "me-and-my-Jesus" gospel,[32] the glitzy church of Christian theme parks, water slides, and liturgical entertainment.[33] It is a grim list. In the world but not of the world; this describes the church's true nature, but it also defines the church's ongoing struggle and, sadly, often its failure.

So, although it is important for the church's liturgical language to reflect its engagement with its cultural environment, it is also important for the church to make every effort to preserve the integrity of its historical faith. In the words of Avery Dulles, "New cultural elements can always enter into the Christian synthesis, but the church's continuity with its origins must always be preserved."[34] This means that whenever the church attempts to reform its language, it will need to keep asking the biblical/theological question, Are these changes consistent with the church's nature to be of God? Are they in "continuity with their origins"?[35]

---

30. A cartoon in *The New Yorker* ([11 February 1991]: 28) shows a couple serving drinks to their guests, another couple. The woman says, "We've been trying on religion to see if it fits, and it does." Martin Marty finds considerable "fetishistic acceptance of secular norms, external standards, and technical triumphs" among orthodox and fundamental denominations, demonstrated by "the 'youth for Christ' interest in hot rods and saxophones, the wearying eagerness to corner all the beauty queens and All-Americans," and "a pious aura of Jesus-saves-ism overlaying it all" (Martin Marty, "Bonhoeffer: Seminarians' Theologian," *Christian Century* 77 [20 April 1960]: 469).

31. Aidan Kavanagh finds that much modern Western liturgical worship "seems to reflect a kind of euphoric optimism unwarranted by a steady hold on reality" (*Elements of Rite: A Handbook of Liturgical Style* [New York: Pueblo Publishing Company, 1982], 99).

32. One study (Louise Bourgault, "The 'Jim Bakker Show': The Program, Its Viewers, and Their Churches," *The Journal of Communication and Religion* [11 March 1988]: 34) finds that the emphasis of the "Jim Bakker Show" is on an "extremely personal deity" with whom Christians "could enjoy four different types of affective relationships: a filial relationship ('God is my father'); a friendship (Jesus is my 'buddy'); a conjugal relationship (Jesus is my lover [for women only]); and a mentor relationship (God looks after my career)."

33. Niel Postman (*Amusing Ourselves to Death: Public Discourse in the Age of Show Business* [New York: Penguin Books, 1985], 124) draws the startling conclusion that entertainment has become the primary mode of public discourse in the United States today, and that television religion and entertainment are virtually indistinguishable. He is also concerned that established Protestant religions may become "refashioned . . . so that they are more televisible."

34. Avery Dulles, *The Reshaping of Catholicism* (New York: Harper & Row, 1988), 50.

35. For a discussion of the complex issues involved in the ongoing work of cultural

Again, the question of being true to historical origins is exceedingly complex (for example, which origins? New Testament? Old Testament? Second century? Sixteenth century?), and not everyone will agree with how it is answered. For example, the Catholic Church is still debating the sweeping liturgical reforms that began with Vatican II in 1962–63. Most liberal and moderate Catholics see these reforms as being a vital step of the church into contemporary society, especially regarding liturgical language; but other more conservative Catholics consider most, if not all, of the reforms to represent a sellout to modern culture, and so a loss of the purity of the church. In the Episcopal Church, too, there has been discussion over whether the attempt to contemporize the liturgical language of the alternative rites in the new prayerbook have accommodated the church's traditional penitential theology to modern social presuppositions.[36] In Central and South America theologians are still arguing over certain reforms produced by liberation theology. Are they grounded in a sound, though radical, biblical/theological tradition, or do they represent a compromise with leftist political ideology?

So the various church bodies often have difficulty agreeing over the questions that arise whenever liturgical reform is attempted. Still, it remains imperative for the church to continue the work of liturgical reform, while maintaining its historical continuity; the church cannot weaken in its resolve to be in and for the world. Indeed, one of the more encouraging developments occurring among many denominational bodies in recent times is the thorough revision of traditional worshipbooks, hymnals, prayerbooks, lectionaries, and other liturgical materials (see Selected Resources).[37] Churches in the United States are currently in the midst of what has been called "a hymn and hymnal explosion," with at least twenty-four hymnals having been published

---

adaptation in the Catholic church throughout the world, see Anscar J. Chupungco, *Liturgies of the Future: The Process and Methods of Inculturation* (New York: Paulist Press, 1989).

36. See Ephraim Radner, "What's Wrong with the New Liturgies," *Christian Century* 105 (3–10 August 1988): 699-702.

37. For example, the major Lutheran bodies (1978), the Episcopal Church (1979), the Lutheran Church, Missouri Synod (1984), the African Methodist Episcopal Church (1984), the Cumberland Presbyterian Church (1984), the United Church of Christ (1986), the Christian Reformed, the United Methodist Church (1989), the Presbyterian (U.S.A.) Church (1990), and the Catholic Church, which provided the impetus for the modern liturgical renaissance with *De sacra liturgia* from Vatican II in 1963.

since 1978 and another thirteen in production.[38] The International
Commission on English in the Liturgy has put the traditional wording
of the most popular liturgical prayers and other formulas into more
contemporary language and will complete the formidable task of re-
vising The Roman Missal in 1993–94.[39] New versions of the Bible
continue to be published.[40] Several bodies, notably the Catholic, Episcopal, Presbyterian, and United Methodist churches, also publish sup-
plementary liturgical materials on an ongoing basis. In addition, the
remarkable "Lima Document," a consensus document on Christian
doctrines, composed under the auspices of the World Council of
Churches from the major liturgies of the world, has been available
for study and general use since January 1982.[41]

So although it is true that attempts at liturgical revision are generally
accompanied by extensive debate over whether (or to what extent)
the revisions may compromise the traditional faith in the interest of
cultural adaptation, the new liturgical materials serve as evidence that
the church is serious about speaking in a language that connects it with
its contemporary culture. Geoffrey Wainwright, summing up the recent work of the liturgical reform movement, comments: "Two guid-
ing stars have been fixed on by the churches in their common search:
they have attended carefully to the church of the New Testament and
the early centuries, and they have tried to reckon with the social and
the cultural circumstances of our time . . . Christian authenticity
requires that it be the *original gospel* which is celebrated in today's
world."[42]

Worship and the World

We have already considered ways in which worship helps express the
church's nature to be the body of Christ in and for the world. Now

38. George H. Shorney, *The Hymnal Explosion in North America* (Chicago: Hope
Publishing Company, 1988), 1.

39. *Praying Together: A Revision of Prayers We Have in Common* (Nashville: Abingdon
Press, 1990).

40. For example, the *New Revised Standard Version Bible,* published for the National
Council of Churches by Cambridge University Press, Holman Bible Publishers, Thomas
Nelson Publishers, Oxford University Press, World Bible Publishers, and The Zon-
dervan Corporation (1990); the *Revised English Bible* (Cambridge: Oxford University
Press, 1989); and *The Bible for Today's Family: New Testament* (New York: American
Bible Society, 1991).

41. *Baptism, Eucharist and Ministry* (Geneva: World Council of Churches, 1982).

42. Cited in J. G. Davies, ed., *The New Westminster Dictionary of Liturgy and Worship*
(Philadelphia: Westminster Press, 1986), 467. Original emphasis.

we need to make an additional point, namely, that the church's worship not only serves to connect the church with its contemporary culture, but also that it affects that culture. It is one thing to say that the church's worship is engaged with its world; it is another to say that the church's worship has the power to influence and shape that world.

Liturgy's Power

Strictly defined, liturgy is "the work of the people," all that the people say and do when they worship God: their prayers, hymns, sermons, rituals, and so on. If this is the case, then "liturgy" cannot be used to describe adequately the totality of the worship experience; because worship is not only what the people do before God; it is also what God does to and with the people. Of course it is important to emphasize that liturgy is something that worshipers create, do, and participate in—as opposed to being merely the action of the clergy. Yet an over-emphasis of liturgy as the work of the people can lead to a kind of liturgical "work ethic"—what the people must do because God requires it, or even a liturgical "works righteousness"—what the people do in order to win God's favor and blessing. Overstating the importance of the activity of worshipers can lead to conceiving of God as more or less passive, accepting worshipers' praise and prayer rather, for example, like a queen accepting the acclamations of her subjects.

In worship it is not only the people who are at work; God also is at work: changing, shaping, gracing God's people. Here is a Call to Worship from a liturgy used in a chapel service at Wesley Theological Seminary:

Leader: This is the place, and this is the time;
　　　　Here and now God waits to break into our experience.

People: To change our minds, to change our lives, to change our ways;

Leader: To make us see the world and the whole of life in a new light;

People: To fill us with hope, joy, and certainty for the future.

Leader: This is the place and now is the time to worship God.

People: Here and now, let us praise God. Alleluia!

The series of active verbs applied to God—"break," "change," "make," and "fill"—appropriately denote how God actively participates with worshipers in a multiplicity of ways. "To change our minds, to change our lives, to change our ways"—all this represents a considerable degree of change! Yet it is a tenet of our faith: God does not passively await and accept our praise. Rather, addressing God becomes God's opportunity to address us. The words of the Epistle of James express this dialogical action: "Draw near to God, and God will draw near to you" (4:8).

So to participate in Christian liturgy is to come under the influence of God to create change: of perspective, of attitude, of values and priorities, of possibilities, of belief. Walter Brueggemann speaks of this power of liturgy as "reconstruction." Liturgy, he says, opens up the possibility for worshipers to challenge the constructs of contemporary culture by providing "an alternative construction of reality which legitimates and makes possible a life more faithful, more obedient, and more joyous."[43] As persons in society, Christians are affected by the influential powers of that society, cultural powers that construct readings of reality. Christian liturgy provides an alternative to those readings, reconstructions that in effect are countercultural. "Every time Israel said liturgically, 'Praise Yahweh,' it said under its breath, 'and not Baal.' Every time Israel said, 'Who is like Yahweh,' it knew the answer is 'Nobody, not any of the petty gods who eat at our life.' Every time the early church confessed, 'Jesus is Lord,' it understood that Caesar had been dethroned and delegitimated."[44]

As an example of the reconstructive power of liturgy, we might listen as James H. Cone, the African American theologian, recalls the Sunday worship of his youth at Macedonia Methodist Church (A.M.E.) in Bearden, Arkansas.

> After being told six days of the week that they were nothings by the rulers of white society, on the Sabbath, the first day of the week, black people went to church in order to experience another definition of their humanity . . . That is why they shouted and prayed and why Reverend Hunter preached such fervent sermons, proclaiming Jesus' presence among them. Those six days of wheeling and dealing with white people always raised the anxious question of whether life was worth living. But when blacks went to church and experienced the presence of Jesus' Spirit among them, they realized that he bestowed a meaning upon their lives

43. Walter Brueggemann, "Newness Mediated by Worship," *Reformed Liturgy and Music* 20 (Spring 1986): 57.
44. Brueggemann, "Newness," 58.

that could not be taken away by white folks. That's why folks at Macedonia sang: "A little talk with Jesus makes it right": not that "white is right," but that God had affirmed the rightness of their existence, the righteousness of their being in the world. That affirmation enabled black people to meet "the Man" on Monday morning and to deal with his dehumanizing presence the remainder of the week, knowing that white folks could not destroy their humanity.[45]

The "meaning upon their lives that could not be taken away" is the liturgical action that, by an act of God, corrects and reconstructs the illegitimate social worldview, and so neutralizes the destructive power of culture.

We turn now to consider ways that specific liturgical acts serve as means of divine action in the liturgical work of the church.

Preaching

Historically, the church has held that the purpose of the sermon is not simply to communicate the ideas and insights of the preacher; rather, the words of the preacher, by action of the Holy Spirit, become a means of communicating the word of God. The function of the sermon is not primarily to communicate doctrinal truths or biblical facts or moral duties or religious admonitions; its function is to communicate the reality of the divine being itself: not knowledge about God but knowledge of God. The sermon, then, represents God's active power, recalling, for example, the witness of the prophet Isaiah,

> for as the rain and the snow come down from heaven,
> and return not thither but water the earth,
> making it bring forth and sprout,
> giving seed to the sower and bread to the eater,
> so shall my word be that goes forth from my mouth;
> it shall not return to me empty,
> but it shall accomplish that which I purpose,
> and prosper in the thing for which I sent it (55:10,11),

---

45. James H. Cone, *God of the Oppressed* (New York: Seabury Press, 1975), 12-13. See also William B. McClain, *Come Sunday: The Liturgy of Zion* (Nashville: Abingdon Press, 1990), 35: "Black Christians have been especially aware that to be Christian is to be 'Easter People.' . . . How many times when the way gets dark and dreary, the road rough and rocky, the problems great and discouraging, the black preacher has reminded a beleaguered and discouraged flock: 'It's Friday now, but Sunday's coming'! . . . [The] bright side for black Christians, and all who believe, is on the other side of the empty tomb, beyond Friday—because Sunday does come!"

as well as the experience of the prophet Ezekiel, when he was directed by God to preach to a valley of dry bones: "So I preached as [the Lord] commanded me, and the [breath/spirit] came into them, and they lived, and stood upon their feet, an exceedingly great host" (37:10).

In the church of the New Testament, though, preaching assumes a character and an importance that distinguishes it from its Old Testament origins. It is the primary means through which the salvation event of Jesus Christ is communicated and made real in human history. Luther reflects this view in the eighth of the Marburg articles. "The Holy Spirit, ordinarily, gives such faith or his gift to no one without preaching or the oral word or the gospel of Christ preceding, but that through and by means of such oral word he effects and creates faith where and in whom it pleases him."[46]

Luke, the writer of Acts, connects the birth of the church with the apostle Peter's preaching (Acts 2). Indeed, as Luke describes it, the first evidence of the gift of the Spirit at the Pentecost event was the powerful apostolic preaching and its dramatic results. "So those who received [Peter's] word were baptized, and there were added that day about three thousand souls . . . And all who believed were together and had all things in common; and they sold their possessions and goods and distributed them to all, as any had need . . . And the Lord added to their number day by day those who were being saved" (2:41,44,45,47b). Yet Luke's view only confirms the high appraisal of preaching set forth by the apostle Paul. For Paul, the normative means by which the redemptive Christ event is made effective in human history is the proclamation of the gospel. "And how are persons to call upon the One in whom they have not believed? And how are they to believe in the One of whom they have never heard? And how are they to hear without a preacher? . . . As it is written, 'How beautiful are the feet of those who preach good news!' . . . So faith comes from what is heard, and what is heard comes by the preaching of Christ" (Rom. 10:14,15b,17).

Clearly, preaching represents one part of the liturgy—perhaps, in the history of the church, the most significant part—through which God effects changes among the hearers, providing an alternative view of reality seen from the perspective of the reign of God.

46. Helmut T. Lehmann, ed., *Word and Sacrament* 4. *Luther's Works,* vol. 38. (Philadelphia: Fortress Press, 1971), 87.

Yet preaching is not the only part of the liturgy in which God works. One of the benefits of the ecumenical liturgical renewal movement is that segments of the church that once thought of the sermon as the centerpiece of the liturgy—in relation to which other liturgical acts were almost peripheral—are now coming to appreciate how all the components of a worship liturgy can serve as channels of God's creative activity and, conversely, that communions in the sacramentalist tradition are coming to appreciate more the place of the sermon in the liturgy.

So, without minimizing the significance of preaching, the context of preaching—other liturgical acts—also needs to be seen as serving God's creative purpose. That is, although proclamation did occupy a central place in the worship of churches in the New Testament, it often occurred in the midst of a liturgical understanding. Even Peter's sermon at Pentecost was delivered to persons who themselves had been participants in the rites of Jewish worship. Following that sermon, the believers "day by day were attending the temple together and breaking bread in their homes" (Acts 2:46a), clearly liturgical acts. In fact, the occasion for Peter's next sermon comes when he and John arrive at the temple for worship: the healing of the lame man at the temple gate attracts a crowd to whom the apostle preaches his second sermon. Further, liturgical materials in the New Testament documents themselves suggest that the primal churches quickly developed their own worship liturgies. Hymns and songs (Luke 1:46-55, 68-79; cf. Eph. 5:19), doxologies (Rev. 4:8,11; 15:3,4), creeds (Phil. 2; 1 Cor. 12:3), prayers (Luke 11:2-4; cf. Acts 4:31; 1 Tim. 2:8), the common meal (1 Cor. 11:17-26), baptism (Matt. 28:19; 1 Pet. 3:21; Rom. 6:4), and congregational responses (Rev. 22:20) in the early church indicate that the sermon was a vital part of a full and rich liturgy.

Blessings

In the traditions of both the Old and New Testament worship, the priest or leader of worship could pronounce a divine blessing upon the worshipers. This tradition is still practiced in many contemporary liturgies, usually at the beginning of the service, in which a blessing from the New Testament is given. For example:

Grace and peace be yours in fullest measure,
through the knowledge of God and Jesus our Lord. (2 Pet. 1:2)

The grace of our Lord Jesus Christ,
the love of God,
and the communion of the Holy Spirit
be with you all. (2 Cor. 13:14)

Benedictions

Again, following biblical practice, some traditional liturgies include a blessing, or benediction, at the close of worship. The person presiding, acting in the name of Christ, pronounces a final blessing upon the people as they go forth to live in the world as the people of God. For example:

May the God of peace make you holy in every way
and keep your whole being—spirit, soul, and body—free from every fault
at the coming of our Lord Jesus Christ. (1 Thes. 5:23)

The peace of God, which passes all understanding,
keep your hearts and minds in the knowledge and love of God,
and of God's Son, Jesus Christ our Lord;
and the blessing of God almighty,
the Father, the Son, and the Holy Spirit,
remain with you always. (Phil. 4:7)

Absolutions

In liturgies that include a corporate confession of sin, the worship leader may pronounce the act of divine forgiveness: the absolution, or assurance of pardon. In most instances the pronouncement is made by the minister in behalf of the congregation. "Hear the good news! The saying is sure and worthy of full acceptance, that Christ Jesus came into the world to save sinners. He himself bore our sins in his body on the cross, that we might be dead to sin and be alive to all that is good. In the name of Jesus Christ, you (we) are forgiven."[47]

In some versions of the absolution, however, the minister will include himself or herself in the pronouncement, in order to avoid clergy-layperson distinctions: "our sins are forgiven" instead of "your sins are forgiven." Perhaps for the same reason the new United Methodist liturgies provide for a congregational response after the pronouncement has been given by the leader.

47. *The Service for the Lord's Day* (Philadelphia: Westminster Press, 1984), 56.

Leader to People: In the name of Jesus Christ,
  you are forgiven!
People to Leader: In the name of Jesus Christ,
  you are forgiven![48]

In most instances, though, the text of the absolution itself, especially when it is based on scripture, points away from the authority of the leader to the divine authority: "In the name of Jesus Christ . . ." For example: "Almighty God, in his mercy, has given his Son to die for us and, for his sake, forgives us all our sins. As a called and ordained minister of the Church of Christ, and by his authority, I therefore declare to you the entire forgiveness of all your sins, in the name of the Father, and of the Son, and of the Holy Spirit."[49]

The Sacraments

Although considerable division exists among Christian churches over the nature of sacramental action in baptism and the Eucharist, most communions agree that, when validly administered by the church, each of the two sacraments represents an action of God upon the lives of the participants. The celebrant's words to the congregation at the beginning of the United Methodist baptismal liturgy exemplify this belief. "Brothers and sisters in Christ: Through the Sacrament of Baptism we are initiated into Christ's holy church. We are incorporated into God's mighty acts of salvation and given a new birth through water and the Spirit. All this is God's gift, offered to us without price."[50]

Similarly, Christian eucharistic liturgies include the biblical Words of Institution that give witness to the work of Christ in instituting the supper historically and in making it effectual in its reenactment. The bread and wine used in the Eucharist and the water (and oil, in some communions) used in baptism are consecrated before being administered, demonstrating that the sacraments are divine actions, not human. For example:

---

48. *The United Methodist Hymnal: Book of United Methodist Worship* (Nashville: United Methodist Publishing House, 1989), 8. On the other hand, the reluctance to accept the authority to make liturgical pronouncements is questionable. See, for example, Grady Hardin, *The Leadership of Worship* (Nashville: Abingdon Press, 1980), 35: "Those [clergy] who feel unworthy to make such pronouncements must reexamine their role as ministers of the keys to the Kingdom granted by both baptism and ordination (Matt. 16:19). Through ordination, the church is authorizing someone to speak God's words with force and clarity."

49. *Lutheran Book of Worship* (Minneapolis: Augsburg, 1978), 56.

50. *United Methodist Hymnal,* 33.

Now sanctify this water, we pray you, by the power of your Holy Spirit, that those who here are cleansed from sin and born again may continue for ever in the risen life of Jesus Christ our Savior.[51]

Sanctify [these gifts] by your Holy Spirit to be for your people the Body and Blood of your Son, the holy food and drink of new and unending life in him. Sanctify us also that we may faithfully receive this holy Sacrament, and serve you in unity, constancy, and peace; and at the last day bring us with all your saints into the joy of your eternal kingdom.[52]

Bless by your Holy Spirit, gracious God, this water.
By your Holy Spirit save those who confess the name of Jesus Christ
that sin may have no power over them.[53]

Consecrate, therefore, by your Holy Spirit,
these gifts of bread and wine,
and bless us that as we receive them at this table,
we may offer you our faith and praise,
we may be united with Christ and with one another,
and we may continue faithful in all things.[54]

This list of liturgical actions demonstrating the action of God in worship is by no means exhaustive; surely God is as able to break through to worshipers, either collectively or individually in, say, the third stanza of the Hymn of Departing as in the eucharistic prayer or the sermon. Indeed, we can say that God can work in all we do in worship; so our understanding of the nature of liturgy is complete only when we acknowledge that liturgy is both what the people do before God and what God does with the people as they worship. Geoffrey Wainwright calls this "the *reciprocal relation* between the divine kingdom and human salvation," which is "both the condition and the content of Christian worship."[55]

The activity of God in worship, then, takes place in many ways and assumes many shapes: it may come as a blessing or a judgment, as affirmation or as correction, lifting a cross from us or placing a cross upon us, receiving us in or sending us forth. It provides a reconstruction of reality that invalidates the claims of prevailing cultures.

51. *The Book of Common Prayer* (New York: Seabury Press, 1979), 307.
52. *The Book of Common Prayer*, 363.
53. *Book of Worship: United Church of Christ* (New York: UCC Office for Church Life and Leadership, 1986), 142.
54. *United Church of Christ*, 85.
55. Geoffrey Wainwright, *Doxology* (New York: Oxford University Press, 1980), 462. Original emphasis.

That God is active in liturgy is both a happy and a frightening prospect, because the ways of God are seldom ordinary and never predictable. Yet all we are able to know about God's ways is all we need to know: namely, that God's work upon us is always in love and always for good. That alone is enough to command our trust.

Liturgy and the World

Because the church is the body of Christ in and for the world, and because the church's worship involves both the work of the people before God and the work of God upon the people, the question arises: What is the relationship between the church's worship and its world? Or, in what ways can the church and its liturgy be described as in and for the world?

In *Christ and Culture* H. Richard Niebuhr outlines five alternative typologies for describing how the church is related to its Lord on the one hand, and to its culture on the other.[56] Although Niebuhr does not specifically address how the church's worship is related to the world, his fifth typology provides the most promising alternative for describing that relationship.

Niebuhr calls his fifth alternative "Christ the Transformer of Culture" or the "conversionist motif," based primarily on the Gospel of John.[57]

On the one hand, he says, conversionists are realistic about the sinful nature of all humanity. In his ministry, Jesus has to face what is deepest and most fundamental to the human race. "He heals the most stubborn and virulent human disease, the phthisis of the spirit, the sickness unto death; he forgives the most hidden and proliferous sin, the distrust, lovelessness, and hopelessness of man in his relation to God . . . [Sin] is deeply rooted in the human soul [and] it pervades all man's work . . . All cultural work in which men promote their own glory . . . lies under the judgment of God."[58]

On the other hand, conversionists hold a positive and hopeful attitude about the future. Their hope finds no basis at all in any intrinsic human strength or goodness, but solely in "the creative activity of

56. Richard Niebuhr, *Christ and Culture* (New York: Harper and Brothers, 1956).
57. Niebuhr, *Culture,* 196.
58. Niebuhr, *Culture,* 196.

God and of Christ-in-God."[59] From the beginning, God has always been and will continue to be in the world. As pre-existent and ascended, Christ also continues the work of creation and redemption, of incarnation and atonement. "The Word that became flesh and dwelt among us, the Son who does the work of the Father in the world of creation, has entered into a human culture that has never been without his ordering action."[60]

As for humanity, the conversionist's perspective is that, although human beings are fallen, their fallenness is moral and personal, not physical and metaphysical: results of the human defection from God all occur on the side of humans, not on the side of God.

> Man's good nature has become corrupted; it is not bad, as something that ought not to exist, but warped, twisted, and misdirected. He loves with the love that is given him in his creation, but loves beings wrongly . . . he produces fruit, but it is misshapen and bitter . . . Hence his culture is all corrupted order rather than order for corruption . . . It is evil as perversion, and not as badness of being. The problem of culture is therefore the problem of its conversion, not of its replacement by a new creation; though the conversion is so radical that it amounts to a kind of rebirth.[61]

This view of God and history places the church in a position of hope, not in the sense of inevitable social progress toward the eventual reign of God on earth, but in the sense that God (or "Christ-in-God," in Niebuhr's words) is able to work in the world for its transformation and that human culture is able to be transformed. For the conversionist, "this is what human culture can be—a transformed human life in and to the glory of God. For man it is impossible, for all things are possible to God, who has created man, body and soul, for Himself, and sent his son into the world that the world through him might be saved."[62]

Although Niebuhr's "Christ the Transformer of Culture" may appear to some to be too optimistic a view of human history, especially in a day when the survival of the human race is threatened by such things as failing ecosystems, it still remains imperative that the church avow some such belief affirming that God still loves this world, fallen though it is, and so continues to work in history through the church

59. Niebuhr, *Culture,* 192.
60. Niebuhr, *Culture,* 193.
61. Niebuhr, *Culture,* 194.
62. Niebuhr, *Culture,* 196.

for its salvation.[63] It is true that we must hear the voices that warn us against idealizing or romanticizing the church's life and work. Its history, as Hans Küng reminds us, is one of fidelity and infidelity, of knowledge and error, in which tares are always intermingled with the wheat: "Its faith is weak, its knowledge dim, its profession of faith halting, [and] there is not a single sin or failing of which it has not in one way or another been guilty."[64] Still, our faith remains not in human righteousness, but in divine grace, a grace that promises to love the world and redeem the church, sin and all. It should be encouraging for us that Paul, in the same letter that exposes a veritable catalog of human sins in the little church at Corinth, never wavers from his conviction that the church, including the one at Corinth, is still the body of Christ.

Bonhoeffer, although acknowledging the painful failures of the church in history, maintained the centrality of its importance to the well-being of the world and history.

> The Christian congregation stands at the point at which the whole world ought to be standing; to this extent it serves as deputy for the world and exists for the sake of the world. On the other hand, the world achieves its own fulfillment at the point at which the congregation stands. The earth is the "new creation," the "new creature," the goal of the ways of God on earth. The congregation stands in this twofold relation of deputyship entirely in the fellowship and disciplehood of its Lord, who was Christ precisely in this, that He existed not for His own sake but wholly for the sake of the world.[65]

So the church's worship continues Sunday after Sunday, not simply to provide worshipers with inspiration or personal affirmation or strength for living or peace of mind; it exists not simply as a shelter from earthly realities or an access to a heavenly home. The church's worship above all is the interaction of God's people with their God, as known in Jesus Christ, through which, by the power of the Holy Spirit, God restores, shapes, and in some way transforms worshiping congregations into a servant people to a stricken world. Geoffrey

63. William J. Carl III (*Preaching Christian Doctrine* [Philadelphia: Fortress Press, 1984], 126–34) connects Niebuhr's five typologies with the homiletical approaches of a selected number of preachers.

64. Hans Küng, *On Being a Christian*, trans. Edward Quin (Garden City, N.Y.: Doubleday and Co., 1976), 507.

65. Bonhoeffer, *Ethics*, 266.

Wainwright concludes his extraordinary volume on worship with these words.

> In worship we take in the outpouring of God's creative and redemptive love, and we offer in return our thanks and supplications. In this personal exchange we are coming into the moral and spiritual likeness of our Lover. This transformation is our glorification in both the objective and the subjective senses: by grace we are being made partakers of the divine nature, and in humility God is being enriched by the requital of his love on the part of his creatures. Our being changed from glory into glory is itself for the greater glory of God.[66]

Measuring how much influence the being-transformed people of God have on human culture is truly difficult; somehow, painful evidences of the fallenness of God's people seem always to compete with evidences of God's transforming work among them. Yet, evidence remains that as the church's worshipers participate in the church's liturgy, they are empowered to influence the world's transformation toward justice and peace, however weakly, and bestow on the world Christ's joy and grace, however imperfectly.

God uses many different means in the work of transforming culture, and surely one of these is the church's liturgy, which can channel a people's longing into an agenda for action.

> Our longing to be whole, forgiven, and to belong is brought to our worship . . . Our longing for God's shalom, for peace and justice, for an end to war and oppression, for all the world to be fed . . . Our longing to extend the church's mission, to serve those in any need . . . But these longings are not left within the sanctuary. Those very longings which come to ritual expression in liturgy become an agenda . . . form our identity, make us who we are as people of God. We bear that identity into the world as instruments of God's peace, as "little Christs" sent not only to proclaim God's reign, but to live it.[67]

The term *little Christs* might give pause. Most people could hardly conceive of themselves as even miniature or microscopic Christs, much less as little Christs. (Psychologists even have terms for people who conceive themselves as Christ in some way or other.) Yet what does it mean to believe, seriously, radically, that the church is the body of

---

66. Wainwright, *Doxology,* 462.

67. Frank Henderson, Kathleen Quinn, and Stephen Larson, *Liturgy, Justice and the Reign of God* (New York: Paulist Press, 1989), 29.

Jesus Christ in the world? What does it mean to live as though God is at work in our worship, changing and shaping us? It must mean, in some way or other, that worshipers are being "converted" to become more like the One in whose name they worship; so that, in fact they are becoming, if not "little Christs," then maybe "little Francises of Assisi" or "little Harriet Tubmans" or "little Oscar Romeros." Through the church's liturgy and with all the "little" people of God, Christ continues the work of transforming culture. The Brazilian hymnwriter, Cesáreo Gabaraín, expresses this in his hymn, "Sois la Semilla" ("You Are the Seed"):

> You are the seed that will grow a new sprout;
> you're a star that will shine in the night;
> you are the yeast and a small grain of salt,
> a beacon to glow in the dark.
> You are the dawn that will bring a new day;
> you're the wheat that will bear golden grain;
> you are a sting and a soft, gentle touch,
> my witnesses where'er you go.
>
> You are the life that will nurture the plant;
> you're the waves in a turbulent sea;
> yesterday's yeast is beginning to rise,
> a new loaf of bread it will yield.
> There is no place for a city to hide,
> nor a mountain can cover its might;
> may your good deeds show a world in despair
> a path that will lead all to God.
>
> Go, my friends, go to the world proclaiming love to all,
> messengers of my forgiving peace, eternal love.
> Be, my friends, a loyal witness, from the dead I arose;
> "Lo, I'll be with you forever, till the end of the world."[68]

---

68. Cesáreo Gabaraín, *United Methodist Hymnal,* trans. Raquiel Gutiérrez-Achon and Skinner Chávez-Melo, 583.

2

Speaking the Language
of Faith

Language matters. This commonplace needs to be stated at the beginning because how one speaks and what is said are not peripheral matters, but are at the heart of human identity and social existence. The fiction prevails all around that words are cheap, that words do not *do* anything: "That's just talk," we say, "words, words, words."

True, words can be cheap and often are. The word *love* on a postage stamp or a bumper sticker is a word without context, so it means little and is cheap. Yet, language can be powerful. Speech is not merely sound waves; words do not merely supply objective data. Rather, language is the power to curse or bless, to bring order or chaos, to create human relationships or destroy them. "Words reveal us. Conceal us. Teach us. Bewilder us . . . Within our brains they give the widest association for often the slightest stimulus. Give lightning sharpness to a cloudy recollection. Evoke tears. Wipe them away. Damp laughter. Cover an ugly act with a pretty excuse. Rip open flesh, then lay balm on the wound. Make more truthful. Make more false. Make more tolerable. Touch with reality. With unreality. Occasionally, occasionally, they ennoble."[1]

Language can be literally a matter of life or death. Amos Wilder is right when he says that "the language of a people is its fate."[2]

---

1. Gustav Eckstein, *The Body Has a Head* (New York: Harper & Row, 1969), 782–83.

2. Amos Wilder, *Early Christian Rhetoric: The Language of the Gospel* (Cambridge: Harvard University Press, 1971), 5.

On the one hand, words can communicate meaning. The language we use, the way we put words together, is the means at hand for communicating what we are thinking. In any serious conversation, we spend considerable energy rummaging through the data banks of our minds searching for the right words—not necessarily elegant or memorable words, but words that will most effectively deliver the message. Whenever I say "in other words" in mid-sentence, I mean that my language has not yet expressed precisely what I want it to; I want my listener to disconnect from what has just been heard and to listen to new language that, I hope, will express more accurately what I am thinking. Yet language does more than transmit thoughts: language discloses identity. How I speak and what I speak about give away something about who I am, what I love, fear, want, believe, value—the ingredients of my selfhood. So, we depend on language to communicate with and to understand each other, which means, in turn, to know and experience each other as persons.

On the other hand, words can hide meaning. Sometimes this is intentional. When what we say might hurt, embarrass, offend, or provoke our listener, we may look for a linguistic means to soften the blow. For example, a politician, not wanting to offend a potential supporter, smothers her political position under a blanket of generalities, or a demagogue uses code words to camouflage his appeal to racism.[3] An airline informs passengers that their seat cushions "may be used for flotation"—language used not to suggest that passengers will be stopping for a swim but to avoid the disturbing thought that the metal tube they are flying in could, under certain circumstances, plunge into the ocean. Bureaucratic language is often used intentionally to sidestep the naming of some harsh or embarrassing reality. Hospitals may refer to death as "negative patient outcome." In popular language, vagrants have become "the homeless" (and comedian Jay Leno has proposed yet another step in the euphemistic progression with "outdoorsmen"). After World War II, the Department of War metamorphosed into the Department of Defense; "battle fatigue" became "posttraumatic stress syndrome." When, for any number of reasons, we

3. Thom Robb (*The Commercial Appeal,* 17 November 1991, sec. A, p. 8), grand wizard of the Knights of the Ku Klux Klan, made public his new political strategy: he will replace racist rhetoric with well-packaged campaigns against affirmative action, quotas, welfare, AIDS patients, and drugs. Potential leaders "will be taught to avoid statements that sound hateful and turn people off."

intentionally do not want to be clear, we can hint or talk around a subject, we can imply or suggest, we can fall back on euphemisms and code words.

At other times we use language that is unintentionally unclear. Bad grammar, faulty syntax, non sequiturs—these may muddle meaning. The use of clichés, platitudes, and jargon, as well as trite and stale words, may get in the way of communicating. Or we may resort to using formal or conventional language. "Dear Sir or Madam," I write. But how can someone I do not even know to be male or female possibly be "dear" to me? Again, we may drift into the casual language of generalities, not so much because our intent is to be unclear, but because speaking in generalities comes easier than speaking in specifics, which requires disciplined and imaginative thinking.

Finally, specialized language—language that includes a technical vocabulary for communicating within a particular field or profession—can be unintelligible to those outside its usage. Granted, all discrete groups need to use code words and technical terms, words that communicate complex ideas easily and compactly. For example, specialized languages abound for football or lacrosse or sailing. The Wall Street broker, the expert in microbiology, and the ghetto rocker all use vocabularies understood only by other insiders. But in order for communication to take place with persons outside the group, some kind of translation, or decoding, might be necessary. Professional journalists, television commentators, and other communicators develop the ability to translate specialized languages into common ones; but everyone depends on this same ability—parents with their teenage children, doctors with patients, police officers with the criminal underworld.

The Language of Liturgy

If language represents the primary power by which a culture establishes or destroys community, builds or undermines a social order, then for the people of God the language of public worship constitutes a primary and indispensable creative power. In Genesis, God creates the entire universe, not with dazzling feats of labor but with words. In the Hebrew religion, whatever a prophet pronounced as "the Word of the Lord" was presented to Israel as an accomplished fact: God's Word equals God's deed. When the Christian community represented by the Gospel of John searched for a title that could adequately and accurately express the unique nature of Jesus as the Christ, "Word" was the theological choice at hand: Jesus was the incarnate expression of God's powerful, creative speech.

Traditionally, many Protestants have called their worship "A Service of the Word," believing that in the sermon, in the Eucharist, indeed, in all of the liturgy, God in Christ is creatively at work to redeem and strengthen God's people. Walter Brueggemann, following Sigmund Mowinckel, speaks of the "constitutive power of praise" in Israel's worship: Israel's liturgy is not merely responsive but constitutive; one's "social life-world . . . is created in cult that mediates the blessing of God."[4] Brueggemann comments: "It does indeed, as every serious pastor knows. Every serious pastor knows as she listens to parishioners that what happens in sacramental activity has a reality that the outside world does not understand."[5]

The language of liturgy matters. True, silence comprises an important place in worship, saving liturgies from wordiness and serving in luminous moments when words fail and tongues must cease. But in worship words need to be spoken. Liturgical language is the means at hand by which worshipers are able corporately to address God. Worshipers speak, sing, whisper, shout, chant, and pray their response to God. Not that this language springs solely from the worshipers themselves; it derives from God. The prayer of the Psalmist, whether spoken or unspoken, prefaces every service of worship: "O Lord, open our lips, and our mouths will declare your praise" (51:15).

Liturgical language is also the means by which worshipers are addressed by God. The reading of the scripture and its proclamation, the blessings and pronouncements, and the words at the Eucharist serve as vehicles for the in-breaking, transcendent voice of God to worshipers: "Thus says the Lord." Liturgical speech, then, is the means at hand by which worshipers both address God and are addressed by God. Worshipers and their God dialogically engaged in expressions of self-giving constitutes a ritual conversation. Because the conversation is one in which God is a participant, its language is more than "mere words" or routine ritual; liturgical speech always bears the potential to be creative and transforming—in Brueggemann's words, "constitutive."[6] In the biblical tradition and the faith of the church, God's Word is event.[7]

4. Walter Brueggemann, *Israel's Praise* (Philadelphia: Fortress Press, 1988), 9.
5. Brueggemann, *Praise,* 9.
6. Brueggemann, *Praise,* 9.
7. This discussion represents a selective treatment of liturgical language. For a more

Liturgy's Worldly Language

The nature of the Christian church is to be engaged with the events of its own time and culture. The church's liturgical language demonstrates its church-world engagement in specific ways. Authentic speech reveals something about who we are and what we believe. The speech of Christian worship needs to manifest that the church's purpose is the same as was its Lord's: to be in and for the world.

Liturgical Tradition and Reform

In what ways, then, does the church speak a worldly language in its liturgies, not in the sense of being the language of the world, but of being a language that engages the church with the world it is in? At issue is the relation of liturgy to both the church's tradition and the church's contemporaneity. To what degree should liturgical language retain the forms of its tradition and to what degree should those traditional forms give way to contemporary expressions? In 1969, when the liturgical reforms inaugurated by Vatican II were being evaluated and sometimes hotly debated in Protestant and Catholic circles, an essay by Martin Marty appeared discussing how the "there and then" and the "here and now" are related to Christian liturgy.[8]

Although one or the other of these dimensions has predominated at various times in the history of the church, Marty argued that they both are essential to the church's liturgy and need to be held together. On the one hand, because the liturgy is Christian, "it will not totally lose the sense of tradition, of history, of past, of shaping event: the activity of God in Jesus Christ remains the center of activities called christian."[9] The "there and then" dimension is what keeps Christian worship from becoming trendy or faddish; without it, liturgical reform becomes a free-for-all. On the other hand, the "there and then" of worship requires "transvaluation" through which the historical realities of the "here and now" are "recast in forms of worship appropriate to their day, forms which will disturb men and signify the saving

comprehensive treatment of the subject, see Gail Ramshaw, *Christ in Sacred Speech* (Philadelphia: Fortress Press, 1986) and *Worship: Searching for Language* (Washington, D.C.: Pastoral Press, 1988).

8. Martin Marty, "The Context of Liturgy Here and Now, There and Then," *Worship* 43 (October 1969): 465–73. The terms are taken from Hannah Arendt, *Between Past and Future* (Cleveland: Meridian, 1961), on which Marty bases his argument.

9. Marty, "Context," 469.

activity of God."[10] If traditionalists "neither recognize the problems of today's culture nor regard positively the possibilities for witness in it . . . then the antique-shoppers of the tradition may well turn out to be nothing more than keepers of the cities of the dead."[11]

The traditional language of worship needs to change—indeed, must constantly be changing—because all living language changes, and because the "there and then" of the church must be influenced by the "here and now" of the culture in which and for which it exists. Yet the changing must be done with discernment and care, so that the solemnity, beauty, and theological depth of traditional speech are not surrendered to language that is merely mundane. In the recent *Bible for Today's Family: New Testament,* for example, "grace" is translated "kindness."[12] Does "grace" equal "kindness"? Does the new word bear the theological weight of the old? The question, as Don E. Saliers puts it, is, "Can we have a liturgical English of richness, dignity, and aesthetic power which also speaks to the realities of daily life?"[13]

Faithful and Worldly Language

Liturgical language is faith language, which means it is special language. The people of God are a distinct people, having inherited biblical and liturgical traditions that have been passed down through the ages. Particular metaphors, images, and symbols for God have been adopted that comprise a unique vocabulary. Gail Ramshaw calls this vocabulary "sacred speech," and so it is.[14] Yet persons who have been a part of the church for a long time can become so accustomed to its speech that they do not notice what a special vocabulary it is that they use. Consider its typical terms of sacred speech: Eucharist, font, psalm, baptism, cross, grace, altar, preacher, Spirit, amen. Or note how the Apostles' Creed, from beginning to end, voices the sacred speech of the church—speech that must seem puzzling to persons unacquainted

---

10. Marty, "Context," 472.

11. Marty, "Context," 472.

12. *Bible for Today's Family* (New York: American Bible Society, 1991).

13. Don E. Saliers, "Language of the Liturgy: Where Angels Fear to Tread," *Worship* 52 (November 1978): 483. This entire issue of *Worship* is devoted to language in the liturgy.

14. That is, words through which God is revealed to worshipers and through which worshipers return their praise and petition to God (Gail Ramshaw, *Sacred Speech,* 12–14).

with the Christian faith. The phrase with which some liturgies introduce the reading of the scripture, "Listen for the Word of God," encodes a particular understanding of biblical inspiration.

The use of a specialized vocabulary in Christian worship is a necessity. For one thing, it has provided the church a historical continuity and theological consistency through the ages. The sacred speech of liturgy is the linguistic norm against which all contemporary expressions must be measured. Further, a specialized liturgical vocabulary is necessary because the single terms in our faith vocabulary stand for the larger doctrines of our faith. Whenever one of the creeds is confessed in worship, the community cannot pause at each faith statement and translate what is meant into the common cultural language. Terms in sacred speech are symbols—code words—that stand for concepts and beliefs.

Still, even though the church of necessity speaks in a unique liturgical language, this language can become idiomatic, obscuring meaning instead of clarifying it, especially in its communication with its broader world. In such instances, the special language of liturgy is an arcane "in-language"—one that only the initiated can understand, a kind of "holy jargon." Because the church exists in behalf of the world, it will look for other words that help clarify its special language, enabling its message to be heard and understood by persons who are outside, as well as inside, the faith.

Because of this need to speak broadly, the church's liturgical speech will be constantly undergoing reform: changing its language in ways that reflect the church's engagement with its ongoing historical context, but at the same time without disengaging itself from its historical and biblical traditions. The difficulty of this process can be observed in the controversies that erupt whenever such translation is attempted. At many points in its history the church has held tightly to fixed, even stylized, liturgical speech, while the language of the world moved on. For example, up until Vatican II, Catholics around the globe, while speaking in native tongues in everyday matters, heard the Mass said in Latin, even though few understood the language. In England, after the Reformation, Protestants used English in their liturgies, but then it became frozen; so that only a few years ago, worshipers might be saying "you are" and "yours was" during the week, but would lapse into "thou art" and "thine wast" in Sunday worship.

A living church needs to have a living language. All traditional liturgical language is itself a product of some culture and to some extent is allied with it. Christians through the ages, for example, have adapted their liturgies to Hebrew, Greek, Roman, and European cultural expressions. Amos Wilder has helped us see how thoroughly the New Testament church, when it first erupted into existence, did so with a "new utterance,"[15]—speaking a language consistent with its new resurrection faith but in dialects the people could understand. Although it retained many of the special terms of its Jewish heritage, it appropriated vocabularies and literary forms from its contemporary popular culture as well, modifying them where necessary and using them to deliver to the world the good news of a new faith. "The founders of Christianity used the languages and idioms of the people: not a sacred or holy language . . . Similarly with respect to styles and forms: these were not esoteric . . . The languages and idioms used by the Christians were those of the wide publics of their time and place. The Christians renewed these in various ways and modified their vocabularies, but there was no flight from the vernacular."[16] As Luke describes the events of Pentecost, the most extraordinary miracle that occurred was that all the tribes from many nations who were present in Jerusalem for the festival that day "heard [the apostles] speaking each one in their own language" (Acts 2:6-11). In Wilder's words, "The common language . . . was itself the medium of revelation."[17]

Using Other Words

How can the church's liturgy speak not only in the special language of its faith but also in the vernacular of its time and place? Primarily through its programs of education, the church will put the sacred speech of its liturgy into other words. In the biblical account of Peter's great confession (Mark 8:27-33 and parallels), the story moves in this progression: (1) Jesus questions the disciples about his identity, (2) Peter boldly professes him to be the Messiah, (3) Jesus orders the disciples to silence, and (4) Jesus begins "to teach them." Instruction follows profession because the disciples' idea of a Messiah was not Jesus' idea of a Messiah. Their accurate confession had to be provided its accurate content—namely, that "the Son of Man must undergo great suffering, and be rejected by the elders, the chief priests, and the

15. Wilder, *Rhetoric*, 5.
16. Wilder, *Rhetoric*, 18.
17. Wilder, *Rhetoric*, 19.

scribes, and be killed, and after three days rise again."[18] So from the very outset, the Christian church explicitly recognized the necessity for catechesis: teaching, instruction. Typically, in the New Testament, although persons enter the Christian faith by confessing their faith in Christ, their ongoing life in the faith depends upon understanding the nature of the faith they have confessed.[19]

So the church's formal and symbolic vocabulary needs to be translated if it is to communicate meaningful content. For example, what does the Nicene Creed mean when it states that Jesus was "of one substance with the Father," or was "incarnate by the Holy Spirit of the virgin Mary"? In order for the worshiper to make a meaningful confession of such phrases, he or she will need to have given them prior thought as to what each stands for in the faith—putting into ordinary language what is in the sacred speech of the creed. This involves a translation, much like what happens whenever a person discusses financial matters with an accountant or a painting with an artist; invariably, time needs to be spent in translation—putting the specialized language of economics or art into a general language that conveys meaning to the nonspecialist. In a similar way, if specialized terms in the church's vocabulary that stand for entire doctrinal constructs are to convey meaning, their various components need to be unpacked and put into common language. One reason persons may complain that they "do not get anything out of worship" is that the faith language used in the liturgy holds little content for them: it is without clear referents. Thus, if the symbolic language used in liturgies is to communicate the realities it stands for, worshipers need to be able to get beyond the symbols and metaphors to their referents; they need to be able to look behind the signs to the meaning of the signs.

The church also has an evangelical concern to communicate Christian faith to persons outside the faith, persons who may be only remotely familiar or wholly unfamiliar with it. Because the church exists in behalf of the world, it needs to be able to communicate with

18. A similar progression is found at the end of Matthew's Gospel, when the resurrected Jesus commands the disciples (i.e., Christian church) to "go make disciples of all nations, baptizing them in the name of the Father, Son, and Holy Spirit, and *teaching* them to observe Jesus' commandments" (28:19-20).

19. For a summary discussion of the role of teaching in the New Testament church, see "Teaching in the Church," in Clark M. Williamson and Ronald J. Allen, *The Teaching Minister* (Louisville: Westminster/John Knox, 1991), 47–64.

the world the mysteries of the faith—to put into other words the essentials of the gospel, the substance of its doctrines. The reason Bonhoeffer so strongly insisted on the need for "the secular interpretation of biblical concepts"[20] is that the language of church doctrine needs to be restated in the common language of society because society depends on that doctrine, because that doctrine is for the life of that society. In one of his letters from prison, Bonhoeffer was critical of Karl Barth's positivist doctrine of revelation, "which says, in effect, 'Like it or lump it': virgin birth, Trinity, or anything else . . . must simply be swallowed as a whole or not at all."[21] To the contrary, Bonhoeffer wrote, "I am thinking at present about how we can reinterpret in the manner 'of the world'—in the sense of the Old Testament and of John 1:14—the concepts of repentance, faith, justification, rebirth, sanctification and so on."[22]

So the traditional faith language of the church needs to be put into the worldly language of its present culture, both for those who are within the church and for those who are outside it. In contrast, the power of faith language needs to be granted—for example, terms such as "Savior," "church," and "cross," may have meaning for children and new converts in the church even before they are understood at a more cognitive level. All symbolic speech communicates at nonverbal levels. Also, because liturgical language is faith language, no translation into the vernacular, no explanation or definition, can fully communicate its meaning. By its nature sacred speech contains the element of mystery, a dimension of Wholly Other, that keeps its deepest meaning and power beyond the reach of rational analysis. God may be experienced through faith, even when God is not understood through reason. Nonetheless, if the church's specialized vocabulary is to communicate its doctrine meaningfully, and if it is to be experienced as constitutive creative power, then it must be studied, translated, and interpreted—put into other words.

Gail Ramshaw has proposed a yes-no-yes approach for appropriating the church's sacred speech. Her schema proceeds in three stages. Initially, the language is simply affirmed as encountered: accepted as

20. Clyde E. Fant, *Bonhoeffer: Worldly Preaching* (New York: Thomas Nelson Inc., Publishers, 1975), 102.

21. Dietrich Bonhoeffer, *Letters and Papers from Prison*, rev. ed., ed. Eberhard Bethge (New York: Macmillan Company, 1967), 144.

22. Bonhoeffer, *Letters*, 145.

holy, the church's witness is trusted as true, and one surrenders his or her life to its authority and power. Then the believer says no to it: hard, probing questions are raised about tenets of the faith, the biblical origins are searched to discover how the language grew and changed historically—and how sacred speech has been affected by human frailty. Finally, the church's faith-language is reaffirmed: the limitations of reason are acknowledged and the mystery embraced, the nature of metaphor to bear the holy is trusted, and the believer again surrenders to the church's word.[23]

The second stage of Ramshaw's scheme obviously places demands upon the church's ongoing work of catechesis. Through its various ministries of Christian education, the church provides avenues its members can travel in order to probe, question, and put into other words the special language of the faith. On the congregational level, churches provide study groups, workshops, seminars, catechumenates, forums, and the Sunday church school as opportunities for open inquiry and serious study. On a broader level, churches provide schools, colleges, and seminaries. Theologians and biblical scholars supply necessary tools—commentaries, dictionaries, study guides, church school materials—that enable persons to study the language of faith. In the worship, ministers may preach a series of teaching sermons: sermons on the creeds, for example, or on the church or the sacraments.[24] Notes and commentary may be included in Sunday service bulletins and parish newsletters interpreting some of the terms in the church's specialized vocabulary.

The church may give meaning to its sacred speech in less formal ways. Thomas Long draws an analogy showing how a church might incorporate newer members into its tradition.[25] Imagine that a family decides to adopt another child. The newcomer enters into the family history without knowing about that history: not catching the family jokes, not knowing who Aunt Bessie is, not having any memory of the family vacation in Florida. The family neither stops talking about its family life in deference to the adopted child nor keeps on talking about it as though the new child had been a family member all along.

23. Ramshaw, *Sacred Speech*, 23–26.

24. See "The Sermon as Teaching Event Today" in Williamson and Allen, *Teaching*, 83–104, for a discussion of the teaching sermon and the different forms it may take.

25. Thomas G. Long and Neely Dixon McCarter, eds., *Preaching In and Out of Season* (Louisville: Westminster/John Knox, 1990).

Instead, the family continues to talk and act like the family it is, "but in ways that open them to this new person who has joined them. Some things will need to be explained; familiar stories will be carefully retold. The family will not abandon its language, blot out its memories, or stifle its cherished patterns. It will simply engage in all of them in the awareness of the presence of this one who is learning the family ways."[26]

The special language of faith is put into the other words of contemporary experience both through informal experiences of community-building, through which persons become more deeply integrated into the life of the church family, and the more formal work of catechesis, through which the traditions of that family are retold, explained, and examined. Because the church exists as Christ's body in the world, it will render the meaning of its specialized speech in the other words of worldly language as an ongoing part of the church's life and worship.

Using Contemporary Idiom

Although Christian worship requires the use of a special vocabulary, it will not depend on that vocabulary. Because worship takes place in and for the world, the church will depend on the idiom of its culture as the predominant language of its liturgies. The voice of the church's worship will not have the artificial ring of a culture from some other time; rather, it will sound like the voice of its own historical present.

Speech reveals identity. Dialects and accents give us away. "You're from the South," someone says, "I can tell by your accent." Someone from the United States touring through Europe may look, dress, and act like a native of the country she is visiting. But when she speaks, everybody knows that she is not from here but belongs somewhere else. For a person to be accepted as a member of any particular place, the person must speak its language.

Because the church's place is in the world, its worship must be primarily in the tongue of its culture. Often it is not. We have already mentioned "Christianese"—a label sometimes applied to worship language that is strongly different from ordinary language; it is liturgical dialect. Clergypersons, sad to say, and other church professionals usually speak it best and most often; and because they are the official

26. Long and McCarter, *Season,* 83.

leaders of churches, the way they speak tends to predominate. In many instances, laypersons who may not be fluent in the special dialect themselves will still defend its use, perhaps out of habit or custom, or perhaps because they, like their clergy, assume that it reflects the special not-of-this-world nature of the church.

Sometimes liturgical dialect is simply language that is dated: for example, Tudor English, with its "thees" and "thous," or the evangelical terminology brought forward from the days of frontier revivals. In other cases, it is the elegant, polished language of a classic prayerbook. In the free church tradition it may be the language of the Bible—speech influenced by the vocabulary (sometimes even the phraseology and syntax) of biblical texts, especially the Epistles. Some clergy speak in a liturgical dialect generally, whether in worship or elsewhere, while other clergy seem to be bilingual, speaking in the vernacular outside worship (or even while making the announcements or greeting persons in worship), but shifting into "the language of Zion" once the liturgy begins.

Sometimes religious in-language is used out of habit or tradition as the recognized way of speaking in a particular communion. In other cases it is used from the belief that it communicates the dignity, spirituality, or piety of the church. But in many cases, it simply offers a practical alternative to the hard work of putting the language of faith into the contemporary idiom—a resort to jargon. As Louis Rukeyser, of PBS's "Wall Street Week," said about the language economists often use: "Jargon is a very convenient shield for people not entirely sure of what they are saying."[27]

Using liturgical language from a different time and culture interferes with the church's effort to identify with its own time and culture. "holy jargon" is not the language of engagement with present reality; in fact, it suggests alienation. When the church does not participate in the language of its contemporary culture, it conveys that it is indifferent to that culture. If that is the case, we have to ask, will the world listen to a church that will not speak in its language?

27. *The Commercial Appeal*, 12 November 1990, sec. B, p. 6. On the language of social scientists: "A turgid and polysyllabic prose does seem to prevail in the social sciences. . . . Such a lack of ready intelligibility . . . has to do almost entirely with certain confusions of the academic writer about his own status" (C. Wright Mills, *The Sociological Imagination*, cited in Joseph M. Williams, *Style: Toward Clarity and Grace* [Chicago: University of Chicago Press, 1990], 10).

Dietrich Bonhoeffer worked on various fronts to bridge the gap between the sacred and secular and the church and the world, and one of these fronts was the language of preaching. "Everything unnatural and artificial hinders the preacher's credibility and stands as a lie in the way of the Word," he wrote.[28] If the world outside the church is to understand the message of the church, then first, the church must come to understand how it, itself, is intimately and concretely involved with the life of the world, and second, must find a new "secular" vocabulary that can be heard by the secular world.[29] "It will be a new language, perhaps quite nonreligious, but liberating and redeeming— as was Jesus' language; it will shock people and yet overcome them by its power; it will be the language of a new righteousness and truth, proclaiming God's peace with men and the coming of his kingdom."[30]

Bonhoeffer provided numerous detailed instructions on the sort of language to be used in worship. It should not be "cultic," that is, the language of religious institutionalism, but "natural" and "genuine."[31] The preacher should not use the language of "the popular orator" or "the lecturer." Neither should the preacher "speak the 'language of Zion' of the pious person" or "the sacramental language of the sanctuary, or that of dogmatics, either." At the same time, the preacher should not " 'let himself go' and use the language of the street. A conscious popularization of language and the use of slang reveal a false understanding of genuineness."[32]

Many contemporary churches are responding to the need to inculturize their liturgical language. As noted in chapter 1, the last decade has seen the revision of scores of worshipbooks, hymnals, and worship resources, as well as the publication of new ones. Although the degree of change varies among the various materials, the linguistic revisions generally include:

1. The modernization of Tudor language and other archaisms (for example, avoidance of "beseech," "forasmuch as," "nigh").
2. The use of gender-inclusive language (although the reforms generally apply to human-language more than God-language).

28. Dietrich Bonhoeffer, "Language in Worship," *Lectures on Preaching,* cited in Fant, *Bonhoeffer,* 172.
29. Bonhoeffer, "Language in Worship," 170.
30. Bonhoeffer, *Letters,* xiii.
31. Bonhoeffer, "Language in Worship," 170, 172.
32. Bonhoeffer, "Language in Worship," 174.

3. The use of race-sensitive language (for example, avoidance of white = good, black = bad metaphors).
4. Sensitivity to terms of designation (for example, "Latino," "Native American," "lesbian and gay").
5. Avoidance of stereotypical language (race, sex, age, class).
6. Avoidance of negative metaphors from physical disabilities (for example, "blind," "deaf," "cripple").
7. Avoidance of positive military and violence metaphors (for example, "fight," "conquer," "war").
8. Expansion of multicultural and catholic perspectives (for example, images and metaphors deriving from Two-Thirds World churches).[33]

In addition to these changes, many liturgical revisions involve a shift away from conceptual, philosophical language and toward a language of imagination, depiction, and concrete experience. For example, The Confession of Sins in the traditional service liturgy of the Lutheran church, "Almighty God, our Maker and Redeemer, we poor sinners confess unto thee that we are by nature sinful and unclean"[34] has become, in the revised liturgy, "Most merciful God, we confess that we are in bondage to sin and cannot free ourselves."[35] "We are by nature sinful and unclean" describes, appealing primarily to the intellect; "we are in bondage to sin and cannot free ourselves" depicts, appealing more to the imagination.

The liturgies for baptism in some recent liturgical revisions call upon various biblical images of water to express the many dimensions of the sacrament: the Creation, the flood of Noah, the crossing through the sea, Jesus nurtured in the water of Mary's womb, his baptism in the Jordan, and, subsequently, his death and resurrection. For example, this is part of a prayer in a baptismal liturgy:

In the time of Noah,
you destroyed evil in the water of the flood;
and by your saving ark, you gave a new beginning.
You led Israel through the sea,
out of slavery into the freedom of the promised land.

In the water of Jordan
our Lord was baptized by John

33. These linguistic revisions will be discussed in chapters 4 and 5.
34. *Service Book and Hymnal* (Minneapolis: Augsburg, 1958), 1.
35. Philip H. Pfatteicher and Carlos R. Messerli, *Manual on the Liturgy—The Lutheran Book of Worship* (Minneapolis: Augsburg, 1979), 18.

and anointed by your Spirit.
By the baptism of his death and resurrection,
Christ set us free from sin and death
and opened the way to eternal life.[36]

So by the use of image and metaphor, the language of many liturgical revisions invites a participation and response by the whole person, not merely intellectual assent. What is said below about linguistic changes in the Lutheran liturgy could also be said about those being made by other communions. "There has . . . been a significant shift in language away from intellectual and conceptual language and toward images that evoke emotional involvement and encourage a more complete participation in the concepts which are proclaimed."[37]

Increasingly, both Catholic and Protestant congregations are accepting the revised ecumenical versions of liturgical prayers and creeds the International Committee on English in the Liturgy (ICEL) has drafted.[38] The ICEL revision of the Lord's Prayer replaces the archaisms "debts" and "trespasses" with "sins," and "thy" with "your," and it improves on the phrase "lead us not into temptation" with a better translation of the Greek: "save us from the time of trial":

Our Father in heaven,
hallowed be your Name,
your kingdom come,
your will be done, on earth as in heaven.
Give us today our daily bread.
Forgive us our sins as we forgive those who sin against us.
Save us from the time of trial,
and deliver us from evil.
For the kingdom, the power, and the glory are yours,
now and for ever. Amen.[39]

The revision of the Apostles' Creed also contains a number of significant linguistic improvements.

---

36. *Holy Baptism and Services for the Renewal of Baptism,* Supplemental Liturgical Resource 2, The Office of Worship for the Presbyterian Church (U.S.A.) and the Cumberland Presbyterian Church (Philadelphia: Westminster Press, 1985), 30.
37. Pfatteicher and Messerli, *Manual,* 19.
38. 1275 K Street, NW, Suite 1202, Washington, D.C. 20005.
39. *Praying Together: A Revision of Prayers We Have in Common* (Nashville: Abingdon Press, 1990), 1. The booklet contains contemporary revisions with commentary for most popular liturgical creeds and prayers.

I believe in God, the Father almighty,
    creator of heaven and earth.
I believe in Jesus Christ, his only Son, our Lord.
    He was conceived by the power of the Holy Spirit
        and born of the Virgin Mary.
    He suffered under Pontius Pilate,
        was crucified, died, and was buried.
    He descended to the dead.
    On the third day he rose again.
    He ascended into heaven,
        and is seated at the right hand of the Father.
    He will come again to judge the living and the dead.
I believe in the Holy Spirit,
    the holy catholic Church,
    the communion of saints,
    the forgiveness of sins,
    the resurrection of the body,
    and the life everlasting. Amen.[40]

Similarly, in most English-speaking congregations the use of the King James Version of the Bible for liturgical readings has given way to more contemporary versions. Although "paraphrase" versions and translations of a single translator are not generally considered appropriate for public reading, consensus versions, such as the Revised Standard Version, are reliable translations written in the vernacular, yet have a linguistic dignity appropriate for worship. More recent versions, such as *The New Revised Standard Version Bible*[41] and the *Revised English Bible*,[42] are even more suitable for use in corporate worship. Although, predictably, all biblical scholars and translators do not accept the translations in their entirety, the new versions do represent a notable step toward putting the Bible into contemporary language: many ambiguous readings in the previous versions have been clarified, a fresher, more contemporary idiom is used throughout, and most important, clarity has been improved for oral reading.[43] The

40. *Praying Together*, 4.
41. The *New Revised Standard Version Bible* is published in the United States by Cambridge University Press, Holman Bible Publishers, Thomas Nelson Publishers, Oxford University Press, World Bible Publishers, and The Zondervan Corporation, for the National Council of Churches of Christ in the U.S.A., 1990.
42. *Revised English Bible* (Cambridge: Oxford University Press, 1989), a revision of the *New English Bible*.
43. For a concise review of these two revisions, see Burton H. Throckmorton, Jr.,

most questionable aspect of both revisions is that, although language with reference to humans has been made thoroughly gender-inclusive, language with reference to God has not. After debating the matter extensively, the translators of each version settled for reducing, not eliminating, the masculine references to God.[44] Worship leaders and lectors who want to read the biblical texts in nonsexist God-language will have to draw upon additional resources.[45]

Because the church's nature is to serve the world in the name of its Lord, to spend itself in behalf of the world God loves, the church's worship must be in a language that is worldly—that is, one that persons outside as well as inside the church can hear and understand. This means that the church will provide ways for rendering its special faith language into the other words of its contemporary culture. Although the church will have to use its sacred speech in its worship, it will depend on the worldly vocabulary of its times. The church will constantly be searching for more effective ways of putting the language of its faith into the vernacular of its time and place—but without surrendering its faith tradition or its orthodoxy. In the next chapter we will consider specific ways the church can share in the language of its contemporary culture.

"The NRSV and the REB: A New Testament Critique," Theology Today 67 (October 1990): 281–89, and Robert G. Bratcher, "Translating for the Reader," Theology Today 67 (October 1990): 290–98. The Bible for Today's Family: New Testament (New York: American Bible Society, 1991) represents the most far-reaching effort to put the language of the Bible into everyday contemporary English, and for this reason it may also find use in public readings, but the loss of much traditional terminology in the translation may make it unacceptable to some congregations.

44. For a rather sympathetic appraisal of the language-gender issues involved in these two versions, see Carole R. Fontain, "The NRSV and the REB: A Feminist Critique," Theology Today 67 (October 1990): 273–80. See also Herbert G. Grether, "Translations and the Gender Gap," Theology Today 67 (October 1990): 299–305.

45. For example, An Inclusive-Language Lectionary (Philadelphia: John Knox Press, Year A: 1983, Year B: 1984, Year C: 1985); Inclusive Language Psalms for Years A, B, and C (New York: Pilgrim Press, 1987); and Gordon Lathrop and Gail Ramshaw, Lectionary for the Christian People (Minneapolis: Augsburg Fortress, Year A: 1986, Year B: 1987, Year C: 1988).

3

Sharing in
the Language of Culture

Creative and powerful, liturgical language is one means through which the Triune God acts upon worshipers, transforming them and reconstructing their understanding of historical reality, which, in turn, affects the events of history. Because the church's purpose is to act redemptively as the body of Christ within culture, the language of the church's worship must participate in the common idiom of that culture whenever possible, rather than depending on the special vocabulary of its faith. In this chapter we will suggest ways the church's worship can share linguistically in its contemporary historical setting.

Using Concrete Images

When Jesus travelled through Galilee teaching the unique message of the reign of God, the people, we are told, "hung on his words" (Luke 19:48). They listened to him in ways they had not listened to their own religious leaders: "He speaks with authority," they said, "not as the scribes" (Mark 1:22). People listened to Jesus because of his personality and unique status, but also because his language, although it was about a heavenly realm, was spoken in earthly terms. Coin, wine, cloth, mustard seed, lilies, plow, money, water, taxes: all are words Jesus used to help people look into the new world of the reign of God. "What is God's reign like? It is like a pearl merchant who found a valuable pearl" (Matt. 13:46); or, "It is like a woman who lost a coin" (Luke 15:9). "Prayer? Suppose one of you has a friend and you go to him at midnight" (Luke 11:5). "Forgiveness? Once there was a rich man who had a manager" (Luke 16:1). The language of parable and story, of metaphor and analogy, of everyday things in everybody's experience, was the language of Jesus' teaching. As Amos Wilder says: "Strophic sayings assigned to Jesus rest on the pungent and figurative tradition of Israel's sages and prophets. Jesus' most down-to-earth rebukes and consolations had the kind of visionary concreteness which we know in an Amos or a Dante. Jesus could see the inexorable verdict of God on his generation in the image of a blasted fig tree, and the overcoming of indurated recalcitrance in the image of a mountain moved from its place."[1]

Typically, students do not expect their teachers to teach in the concrete language of things: it is not the usual language of pedagogy. Neither do worshipers typically expect their clergy to preach and pray in the concrete language of things. The Sunday liturgy often is assumed to traffic in the abstract. Sin, salvation, grace, love, commitment, community, sacrament (and such popular phrases as "accept Christ" and "get right with God")—these are the kind of words more often expected to be heard in Sunday liturgies than the familiar objects of everyday existence.

In some cases preachers and liturgists have to use abstract words, but worship leaders should try, whenever possible, to get around using abstractions, should "flesh them out" into the empirical world of "things" like fig trees and plows and taxes. David Buttrick says that the church's abstract religious vocabulary "may no longer be terribly useful. They are good words, they are our words, and they are convenient words in theological discussion, but because they no longer figure in daily conversational exchange, they may be alien terminology to most people in the congregation."[2] Frederick Buechner, in his delightful book *Whistling in the Dark,* discusses what he terms "algebraic preaching": "$x + y = z$. If you know the value of one of the letters, you know something. If you know the value of two, you can probably figure out the whole thing. If you don't know the value of any, you don't know much."[3] Yet, he says, some preaching is like this. When congregations have to listen to variations of the same old religious language week after week, they might as well spend Sunday morning at home with the funnies.

---

1. Amos Wilder, *Early Christian Rhetoric* (Cambridge: Harvard University Press, 1971), 119.
2. David Buttrick, *Homiletic* (Philadelphia: Fortress Press, 1987), 194.
3. Frederick Buechner, *Whistling in the Dark* (New York: Harper & Row, 1988), 5.

Coming home from church one snowy day, Emerson wrote, "The snow was real but the preacher spectral." In other words nothing he heard from the pulpit suggested that the preacher was a human being more or less like everybody else with the same dark secrets and high hopes, the same doubts and passions, the same weaknesses and strengths. Undoubtedly he preached on matters like sin and salvation but without ever alluding to the wretched, lost moments or the glad, liberating moments of his own life or anybody else's.[4]

The language of liturgy, then, needs to be chiefly the language of experienced life, since experience communicates meaning. The experience does not have to be personal or even shared. It can be experience we have observed or read about or been told about. It can even be imagined experience: the language of metaphor, analogy, and simile, or of story, illustration, and example. Experience can communicate meaning even though a particular event has no direct parallel in the listener's personal experience. If it can be imaged, that is, if the listener's bank of experiences contains enough data to connect imaginatively with the experience being described, then cognition is likely to take place. Our conversational speech reflects that this is so. "I can relate to that," we say, or "I see," or "I know how you must feel," meaning: "Even though I haven't experienced exactly what you have, I've had other experiences that made me feel the way you do."

Liturgical language needs to "translate" the abstract into the concrete. Ideas and concepts will be brought to life by using the everyday speech of people and things, times and places—"worldly" language. For example, if I want to use the abstract word *salvation* in a sermon, I would try to come up with a concrete situation that expresses what I mean by it. In fact, I might even begin by asking myself that question: What *do* I mean by salvation? Salvation from what? For what? By what means? With what kind of result? Maybe I decide that salvation has something to do with "the glad liberating moments," in Buechner's words, above—when I experience that I, of all people, have been touched by God's love and made a member of God's family. If I decide

---

4. Buechner, *Whistling*, 6. See also Fred B. Craddock's comment (*As One Without Authority* [Nashville: Abingdon Press, 1979], 59–60): "A hesitation, almost a fear of concreteness, runs through the history of the church to the present day. We never cease being surprised that upon the death of a saint, visiting mourners discover at his home brooms, detergents, ironing board, worn sweater, trash can, toilet tissue, a can of tuna, and utility bills."

that the family metaphor would communicate well with a particular congregation (it might not with others), I could go on to imagine what it means to be a son or a father: what it feels like, how it makes me act. Or, from another perspective, I might see salvation as being an undeserved and unexpected gift of freedom from the tyranny of my own worst self: an act of God that delivers me from my just desserts. Like what? A condemned prisoner's sudden and unexpected (undeserved?) release from death row? Waking up from a terrifying nightmare? A doctor's announcement that the laboratory tests proved negative and I'm not going to die after all? Receiving a pardon from the judge instead of a jail sentence? Then again, I might see salvation as being the healing of my brokenness, my "sickness unto death." In that case I might turn to medical analogies, or draw on the suggestive phrase often heard in the prayers of African American worship: "Fix me, Lord, just *fix* me."

Sometimes adding a prepositional phrase to an abstract word will at least reduce the abstraction, if not replace it. For example, if in a pastoral prayer I should ask God to increase "our Christian commitment," I might add a phrase that helps describe the commitment: "to work for justice in our city," or "to our church's prison ministry." The point is that *I* will need to know what kind of commitment *I* have in mind, first. If I cannot express concretely the kind of commitment I mean, then I am likely to be thinking of commitment in general—an abstraction that does not communicate an image.

William D. Thompson recommends using his "abstract-concrete scale" to reduce the number of abstract words in liturgical speech. He suggests that we imagine (or write down) a vertical continuum with the word "abstract" at the top and "concrete" at the bottom, and then place a word such as "compassion" at the top of the scale. Reducing that word to mid-level, we might come up with "helping our neighbors in need." Then, moving on down as an even more concrete expression of the word, we might think of "teaching an adult reading class at the Literacy Training School." The purpose of the plan is to provide a step-by-step method for moving from the abstract toward the concrete.[5]

Engaged with its culture, the church needs to reflect the concrete experience of that culture in the language of its worship. When necessary, it will speak in the abstract terminology of its faith; when

5. William D. Thompson, *Preaching Biblically* (Nashville: Abingdon Press, 1981), 67–68.

possible, it will work to translate abstract terms into concrete experience.

Naming the Specifics

A pastor in Alberta, Canada, tells this story on himself.

> "I have a complaint against you, Pastor," said the old brother. He had seemed so happy to see me when he answered the door. "Ah, the pastor. Come on in." But I was barely seated before he wagged a bony finger at me and voiced his complaint.
>
> This time it was Israel's invasion of Lebanon. (The time before it had been the drought and starvation in Ethiopia.) "And you didn't even mention it in your prayer last Sunday," he said, shaking his head. "Not a word. I was disappointed."
>
> He was right, of course, and he started me thinking. What is the scope of intercessory prayer in the worship service?[6]

The language of liturgy needs to specify, or name, by translating the general into the particular.

General language is collective language that travels down the smooth middle road of human experience, avoiding the bumpy particulars along the edges that might shake up the ride. In fact, it is sometimes called middle language. In everyday conversation, general language can be useful. For example, it can be used to avoid mentioning some painful or controversial matter: a patient does not want to talk about her illness, or friends generalize their comments about a potentially divisive political issue. At other times general language is used as a way of being inclusive: a group of people in a conversation will talk about subjects familiar to all so all can participate.

Liturgical language often will be "middle" in both of these ways. Because worship is public, we have an obligation to respect each other's right to privacy: for example, the worship leader's sermons and prayers will not reveal details of parishioners' personal problems, and prayers of confession will be general enough not to expose any one person's particular sin. Further, because worship is corporate, the worship leader will be sensitive to the shared needs and conditions of the community as a whole: her or his language will try to be general enough to be inclusive of the various (and often conflicting) ideologies,

6. William Vander Beek, "Priestly Prayers: Intercessions for the Church and World," *Reformed Worship* 11 (Spring 1989): 31.

political orientations, and social viewpoints resident in the community. Persons who lead corporate prayers of intercession in effect "put words in people's mouths." Being aware that some worshipers become upset or even angry when controversial issues are named, they may fall back on general language to keep peace within the church family.

Yet general language may be used by clergypersons simply because it is a convenient way of dodging touchy topics or situations—a way of substituting caution for candor. Middle language is noncommittal and can become the preferred language of liturgy out of simple fear of controversy. Or, it can predominate because general language is the easier alternative to the difficult work of using specific language: it takes less creative thought to speak both abstractly and generally than concretely and specifically. Still, even with all the potential for its misuse, the language of worship is both public and corporate, and so to some degree will have to be middle language.

Yet, the church is most effectively able to demonstrate its engagement with culture when its liturgical speech is specific. Generic, all-purpose liturgical language tends to be flat and uninviting, but worse, it fails to connect mind and imagination creatively with contemporary realities. The field of journalism recognizes this. Almost invariably, when a news journalist reports on some broad topic or complex situation, she or he will begin with a specific real-life situation. For example, a reporter doing a story on water pollution for a Washington television newscast began: "Welcome to the Potomac River. No, not the Potomac River of song and story. Maybe not even the Potomac River of your own recent memory. Because, today, the Potomac is dying. Over there, along the bank you can see the brackish residue from the latest oil spill. And over on the other side. . . ." A newspaper report on the escalating problem of homeless people in the United States began: "The lanky fourth-grader was ashamed that he and his mother had been evicted from their home, that they had to live for awhile in their car and had ended up in a shelter in Wheaton." News stories like these focus first on one or more specific situations involving persons, times, and places, and then weave in other general material, such as background information, statistical data, and the larger, more complex situation.

Specific language is a language of details. The word *pollution* in the above example does not communicate much: it is one of the code words we hear repeated so often that it forms almost no image in our minds. But "Potomac River" and "dying" and "brackish residue" penetrate our imaginations so sharply that we can almost see, even smell, the pollution.

Details connect us with our world and its events. "Guess what happened to Justin and me on our way to Knoxville yesterday?" my son, Chris, asks me. Instantly I am connected with his experience and am anxious for him to get on with the details. Was what happened good or bad, funny or scary? How did it turn out? I want the details. Here is a paragraph taken not from a scientific journal on communication but from *The New Yorker* magazine: "Details are the stuff of a humanistic perspective. Ambiguous and unpredictable, details undermine ideology. They are connective. They hook your interest in a way that ideas never can. If you let in the details of some aspect of life, *you almost have to allow that aspect to be what it really is rather than what you want or need it to be.*"[7]

Here is an example. I had heard of the AIDS quilt before I arrived in Washington for my sabbatical. I knew that it was a huge quilt made up of single 3' x 6' panels of varying materials; each had been handmade by friends or family to commemorate a loved one who had died from AIDS. I had read somewhere that it required a large area to be displayed. But one Saturday while I was in the city, the quilt was unfolded on the Ellipse across from the White House, giving me the chance to see it. That was when I discovered that I had not really "known" about the quilt and what it stood for at all. It was only when I saw it covering fourteen acres and looked across its 10,848 panels; when I walked among the panels and read names like Andy Baker and Max Robinson and Baby Jessica embroidered or sculpted on them; and when I heard people speaking in hushed voices and saw them on their knees beside names of persons they had loved, softly sobbing, that I came to "know" about the quilt for the first time. That day the details of death by AIDS hooked my interest, and I had to allow it to be what it really is rather than what I wanted or needed it to be.

It is true that the details of that experience were primarily visual, not aural. Still, in a similar way when specific language is spoken in liturgies it encourages us to participate in the experience being described in ways that general language does not. In fact, general language, at least the overuse of it, can serve as a kind of insulation that protects us from sharing in what is being described. So, a petition

---

7. "The Talk of the Town," *The New Yorker* (21 August 1989): 23. Emphasis added.

"for all those who are in need" in a prayer of intercession, or "for the sins we have committed against you, O God, and each other" in a prayer of confession, does not effectually pierce our consciousness or bond us with the realities of human experience. John Killinger puts it well: "It is all right to pray for the poor and hungry of whole nations en bloc, I suppose; there is hardly a way of avoiding it. But I also favor narrowing down the object of prayer as much as possible, and beseeching God for such subgroups and individuals as all the men in Karachi over sixty or all the women going through childbirth in Soweto or all the six-year-olds going hungry in Calcutta. Somehow this seems a little more personal and even more manageable."[8]

Thomas Troeger tells of a more personal experience. While recovering from heart by-pass surgery, during the sleepless hours of the night in the hospital, he would pray prayers such as this:

> God of peace, God of healing, God of life and death, be with the family that was sobbing in front of the elevator, restore sight to the Oriental gentleman who passes me with the cane and the eye patch over his right eye, ease the confusion of the old woman who moans through the night . . . reknit the bones and ligaments of the young woman in the great full leg cast . . . mend the nurse whose back is out from lifting a patient, comfort those who die this night, bring faith, bring peace, bring care through anyone who helps anyone in need wherever they may be. Amen.[9]

Again, this is a personal prayer, not meant to serve as a model for public prayer. Yet it does illustrate how naming the details of human experience can link us to the reality of that experience and draw us to participate in it. In fact, Troeger goes on to say that the reason he prayed this kind of prayer was because "the pain I was feeling was reminding me of *my interconnectedness to all the others* who were in pain."[10]

Because the church is in the world as the body of Christ, it suffers in behalf of the world; it identifies with "the others," the "least of these," for whom Christ also died. The liturgical language that best exemplifies and embodies this is specific language because it names the realities of human experience. We turn now to examine ways

8. John Killinger, *Prayer: The Act of Being with God* (Waco: Word Press, 1981), 73–74, paraphrased.

9. Thomas Troeger, "Creature to Creature," *Biblical Preaching Journal* 2 (Summer 1989): 32.

10. Troeger, "Creature," 32. Emphasis added.

liturgical language can be made specific and to offer some examples. In this section we will focus on the local parish; in the next chapter we will consider the larger communities of which the church is a part.

James F. White says that good eucharistic prayers can be prayed only by a "true pastoral theologian,"[11] yet this applies to intercessory prayers equally well: the presider "performs a representative act for the people . . . Not anyone could do it, only someone who [knows] both theology and the people."[12] A pastor who is in touch with the members of his or her parish and who is familiar with their various primary life-contexts will be able to draw on that familiarity as he or she plans the various components of the Sunday liturgy. That pastor will know that the sermon will not be delivered to "universal Christians" each Sunday but to Margaret, Raymond, the Jamison family, the Farris children, and other distinct persons, and that the "general prayer" must not be so general that it fails to represent the distinct life-situations of individual parish members. This means that the sermon, some of the petitions and intercessions in the pastoral prayer, the prayer of thanksgiving, and to some extent the confessional, will touch on the specific life experiences of persons in the congregation.

In order to do this, some ministers, as they plan their sermons and prayers, mentally visualize the primary everyday environments of their parishioners: factory, playground, office, hospital, retirement home, college dormitory or frat house, nursery school, service station, volunteer center, and so on, allowing what they "see" to influence how they speak in their Sunday liturgies: in prayer intercessions, in the sermon examples and illustrations, in the parish announcements. Others, as Thomas Long notes, survey the congregation in their mind's eye, seeing familiar faces and the lives behind them.

> They see the adults and the children, the families and those who are single, those who participate actively in the church's mission and those who stand cautiously on the edges of the church's life. They see those for whom life is full and good and those for whom life is composed of jagged pieces. They see the regulars sitting in their customary places, and they see the stranger, the newcomer, the visitor, hesitating and wondering if there is a place for them. They see the people who are there, and they see the people who cannot be there, or who choose not to be there.[13]

11. James F. White, "Function and Form of the Eucharistic Prayer," *Reformed Liturgical and Worship* 16 (Winter 1982): 18.

12. White, "Eucharistic Prayer," 18.

13. Thomas Long, *The Witness of Preaching* (Louisville: Westminster/John Knox, 1989), 56.

Still other clergypersons make it a practice to read through the congregational membership roll week by week, pausing at the names of various parish members to consider such things as victories or failures, problems and needs, gifts, special times, good or bad news, unusual experiences or once-in-a-lifetime events, births or deaths, anniversaries, celebrations, troubles, and anxieties. A running list kept of noteworthy experiences parishioners have during the week can, Sunday by Sunday, show up in the liturgical prayers or be mentioned as parish concerns and celebrations.

The question arises: How specific can liturgical language be? Which details should be included? To what degree should liturgical prayers be personal? The answer will differ among congregations, of course, depending upon their size, constituency, and customary practice. It is probably true that in the majority of congregations liturgical speech will not be so specific that it involves mentioning the personal needs of individual parishioners. Yet some congregations provide a place in their liturgies where worshipers may audibly request prayers for named persons and distinct situations. On the one hand, this can be effective when done with thought and preparation: members of the congregation as a whole, not the pastor alone, voice concerns and assume responsibility for each other's care, and the specificity of the names serves to draw worshipers into life experiences of the whole community. On the other hand, if the practice is done casually, it can have the reverse effect: glaring omissions or simply the lack of requests can convey that the congregation is *not* aware of each other's needs and so is not seriously involved in congregational ministry. So in liturgies where a provision is made for voiced prayer requests, the list of petitions probably should be drawn up by a parish committee (perhaps working cooperatively with the parish minister), whose knowledge of the conditions of the full membership makes sure that the needs of all will be named in a systematic way.

Where specific names and situations are not audibly expressed, the prayer leader still can find opportunities for voicing specific rather than general concerns. General petitions for "all those who are sick or troubled," "persons in our community who have special needs," or "our family, neighbors, and friends" (along with the classic "all for whom it is our duty to pray"), are not likely in themselves to induce congregational participation, whereas petitions that provide details or "scenes" do. For example, in her morning prayer, a minister in Memphis once expressed thanks for many of the social agencies in the community that provide various kinds of relief services: "For persons who work with the Loaves and Fishes ministry, as they carry groceries to persons whose homes have burned or who have lost their jobs or who have experienced medical emergencies; for Alcoholics Anonymous and its work of rehabilitation and support among persons addicted to drugs or alcohol; for the people who run downtown soup kitchens and midtown clothes closets; for Omega House that provides shelter and hope for abused children and runaway teenagers." Here are other examples of prayer petitions in the specific language of experience for members of a hypothetical congregation:

- for those who are alone, confined to their rooms: remind them of your presence and send them the comfort of a friend.

- we rejoice with those who soon will be coming home from hospitals, and pray for those who soon must enter them.

- for young people who struggle to resist the allure of drugs; and for others who fight to get free from their addiction.

- for those whose work is dangerous: keep them safe; for those whose work is hard: give them strength; for those whose work is boring: give meaning to what they do.

- for persons who are disliked or who have trouble getting along with others: clothe them in special gifts of your grace.

- for those who go to school, both teachers and students: bless them with a talent for teaching and a hunger to learn.

- we thank you for boyfriends and girlfriends; for those who will listen to us, who like to talk with us on the phone and hang out with us on weekends.

- for our children who attend day-care centers while their parents work, and for their caregivers: arm them with creative love.

- for those who are fighting against harmful habits: break the chains that enslave them; set them free so that they may be at peace with themselves and with their neighbors.

- O God, we seek your creative presence in our homes: strengthen relationships between parents and children, husbands and wives, sisters and brothers; bring peace where there is trouble, joy where there is bitterness, reconciliation where there is division.

- we rejoice with those who have just graduated from college, and with those who have moved into a new home, and with those who have made new friends.

Special attention must be given to the language of corporate prayers of confession.[14] If the sins confessed are overly specific, the results can be negative: the prayers can cause embarrassment to worshipers and seem inappropriate to the liturgy, they can come across as accusatory or judgmental, or they can appear to single out the discrete sins of individual worshipers. For example, leaders of prayer probably would not confess that "we have been unfaithful to our wives or husbands," or "cheated on our income tax returns," or "have fled to the suburbs to escape black families moving next door to us." This level of specificity is better left to the personal prayers we pray alone, as Jesus said, in the privacy of our closets.

Confessions that do not get beyond middle language, however, tend to suffer the weaknesses of all middle language. Confessions such as "we have done the things we ought not to have done and have not done the things we ought to have done" and "we have sinned against you in thought, word, and deed" do not penetrate consciousness or engage us with the realities of life-experience. General confessions do rightly acknowledge that we *are* sinners (as in the tax collector's lament: "O God, have mercy on me, a sinner" [Luke 18:13]), but they do not name our sins or probe into the nature and extent of human evil. It is the same here as with other forms of speech: specific language names and identifies, whereas general language evades. For example, one day Jesus began to talk with a woman at a well in Samaria. She wanted to talk about this and that (especially theology!), but Jesus wanted to talk about "it": not her sin-in-general but her five husbands and her present live-in (John 4:5-30). Although this episode involves a personal conversation and not a liturgical prayer, it illustrates how our sins need to be named. General language smothers the particulars and so, to some degree, skirts the realities.

But because Christian worship is corporate, worship leaders must be extremely careful that the specific language of corporate confessions does not infringe upon worshipers' personal privacy. Sometimes the use of qualifying words when specific sins are named in confessionals helps provide worshipers with the freedom either to include or exclude themselves from the sin named. For example:

- *sometimes* our faith is weak and we trust more in ourselves and our merits than we trust in you and your mercy.

14. See Theodore W. Jennings, Jr., *The Liturgy of Liberation: The Confession and Forgiveness of Sin* (Nashville: Abingdon Press, 1988).

- we *often* have ears to listen to the wisdom of this world but do not hear your "wonderful words of life."

- forgive us *whenever* we put our trust in the mighty weapons of war instead of in your righteousness and justice.

- *some of us* do not look at the signs of poverty all around us; *others of us* see them but do not respond.

- forgive us *if* we put down our neighbors with unkind words or *if* we avoid persons because they are different from us.

- for *any* cheating or crookedness in our work or play, or *any* cutting of corners to get our own way.

Further, the specific language of confessionals will be careful not to imply what persons' motives or intentions might be. There is no certain way for anyone to know what any other person wills to do, unless the person chooses to reveal it. Yet confessions can be worded in such a way that they seem to presume knowledge of why persons have committed certain sins. For example, "Because our lives are riddled with self-doubt, we turn to worldly success for satisfaction" may describe what some of us do, yet it presumes to know *why* we do it. (In fact, the word *because* in prayers of confession has to be used with extreme caution.) So in prayers of confession it is better to describe *what* we do instead of *why* unless it is determined that the motive is as general as the act itself. Notice that the fourth example in the list above reads "some of us *do* not" instead of "some of us *will* not" because "*will* not" implies intention, possibly even a conscious decision to act in that way, whereas "*do* not" only names the sin.

None of this is to say, though, that the specific language of liturgical confessionals cannot also be direct and unqualified. This is especially true regarding the confession of collective sins. The nature of human *sin* is such that a great many *sins* are common to our humanity. In the biblical tradition, collective sins, that is, sins that describe a nation or society generally, belong to all and are suffered by all; so they must be confessed by all. Here again confessions of collective sin will not always have to be in general language (for example, "we are a fallen people," "we have turned from you to serve gods of our own making"), but can *name* some of the ways the nation and culture have failed in the sight of God.

- for eagerness to get the best things for ourselves in this land of plenty, and slowness to share our affluence with people in lands of want.

- for a timid spirit that tolerates evil and keeps silence in the face of injustice.

- nations continue to lift up sword against nations; money that could be spent for food and medicine still is being spent for tanks and guns; while leaders hold summits to talk of peace, they keep factories humming that prepare for war.

- we have trashed entire oceans, denuded entire forests; our skies deliver acid rain, our rivers carry chemicals; your beautiful earth, O God, what are we doing to it?
- you have created us as one human family, yet we are broken and divided; we separate into black and white, poor and rich, socialist and capitalist, labor and management; our nation consists of group against group: disputing, competing, shouting at one another.

The daily newspaper sometimes will carry stories about social evil, often with graphic descriptions that can be adapted for prayers of confession. For example, these two sentences appeared in a Sunday paper in separate book reviews (slightly altered for use here):

The sky is raining acid on dying lakes and forests; the ocean is giving back the filth from our cities; lead is in our water and Alar is on our apples; and we are being smothered by a blanket of carbon dioxide.

Our economic growth is being fueled by waste: extravagant packaging, disposables, planned obsolescence and styling changes, all whip up in us a desire for still more.[15]

These quotations almost beg to be included in the church's painful but indispensable work of national repentance and confession.

Trying to determine how specific the liturgical language of worship can be is not a simple matter, and probably no one parish minister or congregation can make that determination for another. On the one hand, they can guard against a level of specificity that either disturbs the dignity that worship demands or breaches the privacy that worshipers deserve. On the other, they can acknowledge that the language of specific experience does communicate life-realities in a way that middle language simply does not, and so can aim at seeing that the language of specifics is a consistent and distinct part of their liturgies.

Focusing on the Church's Public

On Sunday morning, 10 September 1989, *The Washington Post* began a series of articles describing the monumental drug problem plaguing

15. "Book World," *The Washington Post*, 12 November 1989, p. 3. Notice that the language of these two citations is more specific than the language of my examples above, which makes the confessions more graphic and penetrating.

the city. It began with a story about how the children of drug addicts were victimized, focusing on one thirteen-year-old girl. The girl's mother had been arrested in a drug raid, and after the girl had been taken to a detention home, police officers recovered a diary she had left behind. The news article carried several of the daily entries from the diary just as the teenager had written them:

> *September 1:* Mommy wasn't here. . . . Too many people were running in and out the police were raiding the place too.
> *September 5:* We got some food stamps and they are gone too and we still didn't get no food and it's all my mother's and aunt's fault because they could of saved it instead of spending it on drugs.
> *September 15:* We had a lot of food today . . . We ate everything there was except one pack of oodles and noodles . . . i am glad that we got the food it was soooooooooooooo tasty. I wanted to eat everybit of it by myself. every morsel or crumb of it by myself.
> *September 17:* No money no money I wish i had some moneyfood food I loved to have some food. Clean Clothes Clean Clothes i wish I had clean clothes. A perm a perm I love to have my perm. Room Room I want my very own room.
> *October 6:* i told mommy the police was at the door but she didn't try to do nothing. they busted the door open, it was really very frightening. Everyone was yelling, screaming, hollering, crying . . . I know for a fact everyone is not going to have a good nights sleep. I wish I was never born.[16]

Earlier that morning I had planned to visit the Church of the Savior in the District, but I was so disheartened by the article that I considered not going to church at all. Yet later, I found myself somehow on a city bus headed for midtown Washington, with words from the girl's diary running through my head like a chant:

> No money no money I wish I had some money
> Food food I loved to have some food.
> Clean Clothes Clean Clothes i wish i had clean clothes.
> A perm a perm i love to have my perm.

At the church, worship began. Early in the liturgy, Gordon Cosby, the pastor, included this petition in his pastoral prayer: "O God, bless this city, especially this city's children—like the teenage girl we read about in this morning's *Post.* O God, save these children. Help their mothers. We mourn for them. Bless us in our mourning." He went

16. *The Washington Post,* 10 September 1989, sec. A, p. 22.

on to ask God to lead the city's leaders—and the rest of us—in efforts to end the scourge of drugs in Washington and throughout the nation and to care for its victims.

Here is an example of the church speaking in the language that reflects the conditions that exist in the society of which it is a part.[17] The Christian faith has always affirmed not only that God *was* in Christ reconciling the world to Godself, but that God *is* in the world, still doing the work of reconciliation. The gospel *was* made incarnational through the ministry of Jesus Christ; the gospel *is being* made incarnational through the ministry of the church of Jesus Christ. As God *once* empowered the earthly ministry of Jesus in the world by the Holy Spirit, God *now* empowers the earthly ministry of the church in the world by that same Spirit.

It follows that the way the church speaks in its worship will reflect the circumstances of its time in history. Its preaching, its praying, and its singing will have to do not only with religious and spiritual matters or with matters of its own institutional life, but with matters of the world it is incarnational *for*. Yet, this is not always the case. A cartoon in *The New Yorker*, which occasionally lampoons the foibles of modern up-scale New Yorkers, shows a clergyman, bedecked in ecclesiastical finery, speaking from a pulpit surrounded by Gothic columns. He says: "Good morning. With a touch of fall in the air, I'm happy to welcome you back from summer distribution in the Hamptons, Bay Head, Nantucket, Chatham, and Northeast Harbor, and to reunite our diverse community—some in preppy garb, some in executive dress, some in the Ivy League look, and some in Wasp attire. My sermon this morning was inspired by Scripture from our 1928 Book of Common Prayer."[18] Although the cartoon may not be entirely fair (how many ministers are still following the 1928 Prayerbook?), it clearly represents a secular commentary on the church's tendency at times to speak in a liturgical language that is discrete and distant from its own time (except for, in this case, the greeting!).

Maybe a better example would be an incident that William Muehl describes.[19] Once, when he was invited to be the guest speaker at a

17. For a discussion of the church in relation to its public, see James W. Fowler, *Weaving the New Creation: Stages of Faith and the Public Church* (San Francisco: Harper San Francisco, 1991).

18. *The New Yorker* (2 October 1989): 39.

19. At that time, Professor of Homiletics at Yale Divinity School.

church in New York City, he was asked by the rector of the church to sit in on a men's church school class on ethics in business, led by the rector. Although the class was made up of a dozen prominent New York businessmen, the discussion, it seemed to Muehl, was remarkably dull and surprisingly thin. A week later, back home, he received a thank-you letter from a man who had been a part of that class; and at the bottom was this handwritten postscript: "I'd hate to have you think that the men in this church are as stupid as we must have sounded in the rector's class. But the truth is that if we ever told that nice little man the *real* ethical dilemmas we face every day at the office, it would break his heart."[20]

True, this incident took place in a church school class and not in the church's worship, but is it not likely that, if the rector's conversation in the unstructured atmosphere of a classroom was so out of touch with the circumstances of the business world, then his liturgical speech in the more structured environment of worship would be as well— or even more so? After all, it is not as if it were necessary for the rector himself to have been knowledgeable of all the thorny ethical questions associated with today's complex world of business in order for the classroom discussions to have been more substantial. But what would have been necessary is for the ethical issues of the real business world to be considered at least allowable into the discussions, but even better, welcome. The businessmen should have been able to assume that their ethical dilemmas, along with all other matters of social reality, *belong* in the church's discussions. One would think that at some point the businessmen would have heard from their church that neither it nor its clergy need to be shielded from the realities of life in the world, because the church represents the incarnational gift of God to that world. How can the church effectively give the gifts of God to a world the empirical realities of which will not be entertained in its language?

This leads us to consider that sometimes it is what persons perceive the nature of the church to be that determines the language the church will speak. For example, if a person thinks of the church primarily as a refuge from the harsh realities of everyday life, then speaking of these realities in sermon and prayer (or to sing of them in hymns) might be considered intrusive, even sacrilegious. Or if someone understands the church's purpose to be primarily providing peace of

20. William Muehl, *Why Preach? Why Listen?* (Philadelphia: Fortress Press, 1986), 14.

mind, personal experiences of God's presence, and supporting relationships with other Christians, then the language of contemporary social problems in the liturgy could be regarded as out of place as, say, a dirge at a garden party.

Some authorities are saying that the strong sense of individualism that exists in a large segment of today's church helps to influence its liturgical language toward social indifference. That a fierce individualism has seized much of Christendom in the United States can hardly be disputed. For example, Robert Hovda comments:

> Attention to the individual is one of the beauties of human evolution, for which we must all be grateful and in which Judaism and Christianity have played a seminal part. The individualism . . . however, has become an absolute, an idol, destroying the human capacity for love, solidarity, and reconciliation, and reducing the human thirst for justice to private dimensions. This is not evolution or progress, but insanity. There is no point in individual dignity and freedom if the necessary community of reconciliation, common support and action is lost.[21]

The authors of the popular book *Habits of the Heart: Individualism and Commitment in American Life* have documented how individualism is affecting culture in the United States generally, including religious institutions.[22] The study details how many persons in contemporary culture consider religion to be a matter of individual preference, only marginally connected with the institutional church or even with society as a whole. The authors cite a Gallup poll taken in the United States in 1978 in which 80 percent of people surveyed said that individuals should arrive at their own religious beliefs "independent of any churches or synagogues."[23] Church affiliation, if any, is strictly a matter of personal choice, since a personal relationship with God "transcends any involvement in any particular church."[24] A 1988 poll shows that the situation has not changed: "Supported by related findings on Americans' beliefs and practices, [the] results suggest a growing trend toward religious privacy."[25]

---

21. Robert W. Hovda, "The Amen Corner," *Worship* 65 (January 1991): 71.

22. Robert Bellah et al., *Habits of the Heart: Individualism and Commitment in American Life* (Berkeley: The University of California Press, 1984).

23. Bellah, *Habits,* 228.

24. Bellah, *Habits,* 228.

25. George Gallup, Jr., *100 Questions and Answers: Religion in America* (Princeton, N.J.: Princeton Research Center, 1989), 66. In this poll seventy-six percent nationwide said that "a person can be a good Christian or Jew if he or she doesn't attend church or synagogue" (76).

Robert Bellah and his colleagues also found that, coupled with this hyper-individualism is a strong subjectivism among Christians in the United States, that is, a predominant concern for inner personal spirituality.[26] Even in evangelical circles the biblical language of sin and redemption is often transformed into "an idea of Jesus as the friend who helps us find happiness and self-fulfillment."[27]

The combination of individualism and subjectivism in popular religion often results in the understanding of worship as the means by which God's blessings are made available to individuals and of the church as a community where individuals support each other and share warm and intimate feelings. In such cases worship liturgies generally become person-centered and introverted, designed to provide personal affirmation and assurance—in effect, therapy.

There is no need to argue that there are degrees of legitimacy to these and other conceptions of the church's nature; many valid expressions of what the church is and what its ministries ought to be exist. Certainly such qualities as individuality, inner experience, intimacy, and personal piety rightfully occupy a place in the church's life, particularly in its worship. However, it is when they become emphasized (in some cases, absolutized) to the point of crowding out other contrasting qualities that complete and balance them, that authentic worship becomes adversely affected. Any conception of what the church is must include a description of in what ways the church is related to its world, its contemporaneous public. Any theology that conceives the church as being in some way extraneous to secular society or indifferent to the issues of the world fails at taking seriously enough the fundamental nature of the church to be the body of Christ in and for the world. Introverted and self-absorbed ecclesiologies serve to draw the church away from its world mission and to shield it from the realities of its historical existence, which takes us back to the businessmen's church school class in William Muehl's story. David Buttrick puts it this way: "Instead of reaching out into the world and daring to name God, the church has tried to bus the world into its buildings where the Bibles are."[28] But what the church ought to do,

26. Bellah, *Habits*, 232.

27. Bellah, *Habits*, 232. For a summary of individualism and subjectivism in the contemporary church (especially in the Catholic church), see M. Francis Mannion, "Liturgy and the Present Crisis of Culture," *Worship* 62 (March 1988): 98–123.

28. "Afterglow," *Academy Accents* 5 (August 1989): 5.

he says, is to "proclaim a Jesus who can not only move in the personal heart but who can begin to transform the cultural mind of the earth."[29]

In a similar way, Parker J. Palmer, in the stirring conclusion of his study of the church's connections with its public, counsels the church not to "resist the inward turn of American spirituality on behalf of effective public action," but, instead, to "*deepen and direct and discipline that inwardness in the light of faith* until God leads us back to a vision of the public and to faithful action in the public's behalf."[30]

So although an important part of the church's purpose is to care for itself, that is, to pray for, heal, share with, and experience God's presence in the midst of each other, it is also the church's purpose to direct its vision outward upon all the others, to "go public," in Palmer's words.[31] The church practices its ministry of outreach in numerous ways: through relief ministries, social action agencies, and missions programs, but also through speaking a public language in its worship, one that reflects the realities of the prevailing culture.

We pause now to ask the question, How does this happen? In what ways does the church's speaking in the language of its contemporaneous public help strengthen its ministry of social outreach? Using the experience at the Church of the Savior as a point of reference, we will suggest five ways.

1. It lays before God instances of human need and suffering that cry out to God for action. To be sure, there is much about intercessory prayer that we do not and cannot know. We know that it is not the same as magic: naming a request before God does not immediately and inevitably bring it to pass. Yet we believe that intercessory prayer is more than empty ritual, or a mental exercise, or the practice of telepathy or autosuggestion. The faith of the church historically has affirmed that prayer for others in some way *affects*, that it enlists heavenly power in behalf of earthly conditions. The Bible itself is the source of this belief: although it does not explain how intercessory prayer works or answer all our questions about it, the biblical view is that to petition God in faith is not merely to ask but also to *act* (for example, Ps. 91:15; Isa. 58:9; 65:24; Luke 11:9; John 15:7; Acts 4:31). Peace activist Walter Wink contends that biblical evidence exists that

29. "Afterglow," 5.

30. Parker J. Palmer, *The Company of Strangers* (New York: Crossroad, 1981), 156. Original emphasis.

31. Palmer, *Strangers*, 156.

God wants to be opportuned: Abraham haggling with God in behalf of Sodom [Gen. 18], Moses refusing to let God destroy Israel [Exod. 32:7-14], Jesus' parable about the persistent widow confronting the unjust judge [Luke 18:1-18]. "Praying is rattling God's cage and waking God up and letting God free and giving this famished God water and this starved God food and cutting the ropes off God's hands and the manacles off God's feet and washing the caked sweat from God's eyes and then watching God swell with life and vitality and energy and following God wherever God goes."[32] Prayer is not merely to ask; it is to participate with God in acting against evil and in establishing good. Intercessory prayer "changes what is possible to God . . . A new force field appears that hitherto was only potential, because of a lack of faith. The entire configuration changes as the result of the change of a single part. An aperture opens in the praying person, permitting God to act without violating human freedom. The change in one person thus changes what God can thereby do in that world."[33]

To invoke God to come to the aid of children of drug addicts, for example, is to bestow on these children an act of God. The church prays for them and for other instances of human suffering for the same reason and in the same faith that it prays for members of its own community: it believes that to pray for them is to bless them in some way with God's care.

2. It gives witness to the church's engagement with the realities of its social existence. As we have seen, our language divulges who we are: what we think about, what we believe, what we are like. If the language of the liturgical prayers, sermons, and hymns of our worship focus on the inner life and interests of the community to the neglect of the needs of the larger public, then it betrays that the church is self-preoccupied, maybe even self-absorbed. In that event, the worshiping community has become exclusive and insular; the "Prayers of the People" have become, in effect, the "Prayers of Our People." However, if the language of a worshiping community stretches out to include the life situations of persons outside the community, then it betrays that it is responsible for and is responding to the larger family of God. Speaking in such language is an effective way for the church to "go public," and helps to contradict the parochialism operative in our

---

32. Walter Wink, "History Belongs to the Intercessors: Co-creating with God through Prayer," *Sojourners* 19 (October 1990): 14.
33. Wink, "Intercessors," 13.

society and in many churches, as discussed above. Naming the plight of the teenage girl in the pastoral prayer at the Church of the Savior brought the shocking reality of her situation into worship and sent the prayers of the people out from worship into that reality.

3. It is representative of the larger needs and conditions of our world culture. It is obvious that intercessory prayers cannot name before God the multiplicity of needs that exist throughout the world. Of necessity, persons who write prayer intercessions have to be both selective and summary. Yet, specific petitions are also representative: that is, they stand for and embody a range of social need far beyond the ones expressly named. A single explicit petition can engage the praying congregation with larger implicit concerns. For example, the prayer for the victimized teenage girl engaged the worshipers with the larger problems of society, the drug culture, rampant poverty, the breakdown in family structures, and the deplorably inadequate state of public welfare services.

4. It invites worshipers to participate in the prayer. As we have seen earlier, unlike abstract and general language, which tends not to penetrate consciousness, concrete and specific language induces the participation of listeners into what is being spoken. Language that is current does so as well. Persons are concerned about what is going on around them; it is of interest to them, it matters. So language about our contemporary public sparks interest and invites participation. In worship all liturgical prayers "belong" not solely to the persons who voice them; they belong to the whole assembly because they represent the concerns of the whole assembly, which, in turn, gives its assent with the unison "amen." So although a general petition, for example, "for those who are victims of the drug culture," might invite worshipers to "pray with" the leader, the explicit reference to "the teenage girl we read about in the morning's *Post*" immediately resurrects recent thoughts and emotions in worshipers, inducing them to participate more intensely in the prayer. (Incidentally, most members of that congregation probably would have read the morning's *Post*.)

5. It effects changes in the lives of the praying congregation. The popular saying "Prayer changes things" is true, even when reduced to bumper-sticker form: prayer does change things, and one of the things it changes is the nature of the one who prays.[34] Intercessory

34. For example, the preface to the Alternative Service Book of the Church of England: "Christians are formed by the way in which they pray" (cited in Janet Morley and Hannah Ward, *Celebrating Women* [Wilton, Conn.: Morehouse-Barlow, 1987], 2).

prayers "are not recommendations to God as to how He should behave in the world; on the contrary, they are my commitment for the world before God, my surrender to God and my adoption by God into His service.[35] It is impossible to pray sincerely, intensely, and incessantly for something and to remain indifferent to it. As persons pray over something or someone, they open themselves up to a divine influence that transforms their attitudes and builds sympathies and commitments. Abraham Lincoln is supposed to have said, "It is impossible to pray for your enemy and hold him long as your enemy." Similarly, it is impossible to pray for persons who are victims of social evil, or who have not experienced new life in Jesus Christ, or who suffer from any of the many forms of human deprivation and not become involved in ministry to them.

Obviously this means that although it is important to pray, it is even more important to pray rightly. The shape and content of our prayers constitute another instance where liturgical language matters. Because how we pray helps to determine what we become, leaders of liturgy dare not treat their liturgical prayers with indifference. Prayers of worship that are consistently in the language of the church's contemporaneous public will influence the congregation to participate in ministries to that public. It is not a coincidence that the members of the Church of the Savior, whose liturgical language is consistently connected with its public, is energetically involved in programs of social ministry. Further, the more a church speaks in the voice of its contemporaneous public, the more it will help confound the over-emphasis on individualism and subjectivism endemic to our society. Introducing social needs into worship liturgies helps redirect attention away from personal self-interest toward a social consciousness.

Although much social liturgical language will center on the troubles and needs of our world, much of it also can center on its blessings and achievements. Worshipers can celebrate events and circumstances they interpret to be evidences of God's presence in the world. The following quotation from Sallie McFague became a prayer for a Sunday's liturgy: O God, we give thanks for your love as we see it "in the teacher who gives extra time to the slow or gifted student, in the social worker whose clients are drug-addicted pregnant women, in

---

35. Vilmos Vajta, "Worship in a Secularized Age," *Worship and Secularization,* ed. Wiebe Vos (Geneva: World Council of Churches, 1970), 77.

the librarian who lovingly restores old books . . . in the owner of the local supermarket who employs ex-juvenile delinquents, in the politician who supports more funds for public education, in the botanist who catalogues new strains of plants, in rock stars who give their talents to famine relief."[36] Although the news media tend to focus on tragedy and social corruption, almost every day's news brings accounts of goodness in our world as well, providing evidences of divine grace and reasons for hope. The language of worship will find ways to celebrate such signs of God's active presence in the world.

The remainder of this chapter will consider ways the church's worship can speak in the language of its contemporaneous public, particularly in its sermons, prayers, and hymns.

Timely Sermons

Martin Luther once wrote, "If you preach the Gospel in all its aspects with the exception of the issues that deal specifically with your time, you are not preaching the Gospel at all."[37] Clearly the sermon is one important place in the Sunday liturgy where the church is able to manifest its involvement with the events of its contemporary culture. The preacher can preach contextually; that is, as the preacher interprets the biblical text, current conditions in national and world affairs can be given their biblical and theological referents. Since the church exists in behalf of the world, the preacher will consistently ask of the text such questions as: How does this text impinge upon the life in today's world? How are the constructs of reality provided us by today's society reconstructed when viewed through the lens of this scripture?

There are, however, certain dangers in this approach. The pulpit must not serve as a sounding board for the preacher's favorite social or political ideas. The preacher needs to avoid speaking repetitively about a limited number of social conditions (such as racism, poverty, war) to the exclusion of others, giving the impression that this or that concern is the preacher's "thing." The preacher will need to be selective: each sermon cannot take on the world and its problems. Then, in cases

36. Sallie McFague, *Models of God: Theology for an Ecological, Nuclear Age* (Philadelphia: Fortress Press, 1987), 121, cited in James W. Fowler, *Weaving the New Creation: Stages of Faith and the Public Church* (San Francisco: Harper San Francisco, 1991), 71.

37. Cited in *PeaceWork,* Baptist Peace Fellowship (November-December 1989/January-February 1990): 21.

where the biblical text or the sermon topic do not naturally connect with current events, the connections should not be force-fed into the sermon.

Still, the empirical data arising from contemporary events most effectively engages the biblical message with life in the world. Many of these events will come from the familiar environs of the church and the local community. Others will come from the national and international scenes of politics, economics, and social welfare. So on some occasions, the preacher will assume the responsibility of the prophets to interpret the times in the light of God's sovereign righteousness: perhaps, like Amos, addressing the ways nations "oppress the poor and crush the needy," or like Isaiah, bearing biblical witness against modern forms of idolatry. At other times the preacher will help the congregation consider ways of serving in its role of shepherd: for example, in ministry to persons who have suffered the ravages of hurricane or earthquake or terrorist bombing. Still again, the preacher will speak as an agent of the reign of God, serving as an advocate in behalf of the millions of marginalized persons society labels with the suffix "less": the homeless, jobless, fatherless, powerless, hopeless— but for whom all aspects of existence are in some way "less."

Even sermons that do not explicitly address social conditions or world events can use the language of the contemporaneous public in illustrations, examples, and analogies. For example, a sermon on a text that focuses on human greed might look for modern expressions of greed: on the level of personal morality (obsessive material consumption or the drive to acquire and possess), or on a larger systemic level (evidences from television commercials, game shows, and advertisements, or the exploitation of the environment for profit, or political bribery and payoffs). Or coming from the other side of the issue, the sermon might draw examples from current practices of generosity: persons who volunteer their time and sacrificially give money for good causes, or the work of such agencies as Habitat for Humanity and the United Way, or examples of a national social conscience: ADC (Aid to Dependent Children), Medicare and Medicaid, WIC (Women, Infants, and Children). If today we can think of biblical miracles of healing as occurring primarily through the medical sciences, can we not also think of other biblical forms of God's providence as occurring through social service agencies?

So the proclamation of the Word is one place in the liturgy where the church can speak in the language of its contemporaneous public.[38]

38. As helpful resources on this subject, see William K. McElvaney, *Preaching from*

Preachers will be alert and observant, sensitive to the events around them and how they might be interpreted homiletically. Granted, this places considerable pressure on the preacher to be both knowledgeable about world affairs and faithful to the biblical text. Yet, at least since the days of the prophets, when has this not been so? Karl Barth's well-known advice to preachers applies here: we preach with the Bible in one hand and the newspaper in the other.

However, a caution might be in order: few secular news media show concern for interpreting news events from the perspective of the church—if anything, they are more likely to be spokespersons for the interests of owners and advertisers. News anchors frequently use "we" and "our" when referring to the United States. The media's North American bias is so strong that coverage of Two-Thirds World countries is minimal unless events in those countries are spectacular or in some way affect the United States. Norman Solomon, of Fairness and Accuracy in Reporting (FAIR), says that networks and newspapers in the United States have become so compliant toward corporations and government that they present "mythology that masquerades as reporting."[39] Because preachers must speak in the language of their social public, it is essential that they read—and encourage parishioners to read—religious periodicals whose aim is to report world events objectively and interpret them biblically/theologically (for example, *Sojourners* and *Christianity and Crisis*). See also "Religious News Periodicals" in the Selected Resources at the end of this volume.

Worldly Events in Prayers

A friend once related an experience of the previous Sunday. He was attending the 7:30 Morning Prayer service at Calvary Episcopal Church in Memphis on 13 August 1989. In the Prayers of the People that morning, the prayer leader included a petition "for the saints and faithful departed," and then read a list of names of persons who had died. The last name on the list was the name of Mickey Leland, the Democratic congressman from Texas. He was one of those rare congresspersons who is as eager to serve the world as a congressional

---

Camelot to Covenant (Nashville: Abingdon Press, 1989), especially chapter 4, "Preaching from Global Consciousness," and Arthur Van Seeters, ed., *Preaching as a Social Act* (Philadelphia: Westminster Press, 1987).

39. Cited in *The Commercial Appeal,* 24 September 1991, sec. B, p. 2.

district. He was a humanitarian, an angel of mercy to the world's poor and hungry. In fact, on August 7, just before his death, Leland had been on a mission of mercy to the Fugnido refugee camp, a squalid place in Ethiopia near the Sudanese border, when his plane abruptly vanished from the radar screens. On Wednesday the plane's wreckage was spotted near the top of Tamsi mountain, but the fate of the passengers remained unknown until early Sunday morning. My friend first learned that Leland was dead when his name was read as one of the "faithful departed" at that early service.

This incident illustrates how liturgical language can connect the worship of the church with events of the world. It is an example of the prayers of the liturgy being said with "the newspaper in one hand and the prayerbook in the other," to paraphrase Barth's remark. But more important, my friend experienced something more: the "theological context the death of Mickey Leland was placed in helped us understand and accept that loss in an altogether different way than if we had only read about it in the morning's paper."

The liturgical prayers of the people at worship can often be the means by which events of life-in-the-world are given their proper theological context. It is true that Christian believers on their own can interpret theologically the world events they read or hear about. But the common prayers of a people at worship provide a unity of concern, a shared experience of responding to events, that generally is not experienced in a purely individual response. The presence of others around us, with us in corporate prayer, affects the thoughts and feelings we experience in response to the life situations named in the prayer. The unison "amen" strengthens and deepens what we experience whenever we say the "amen" alone.

The language of our contemporary public can be woven into liturgical thanksgivings, intercessions, and petitions in a number of ways. (Prayers of confession, as we have seen, require a more general language, and so are not as suitable.) Here are some examples.

The pastor of a United Methodist church occasionally reads several headlines from the morning's newspaper (visible to the congregation), and then says, "Let us make our intercessions before the Lord." At other times, members selected from the congregation will stand at their pews and read a headline (given to them in advance). The news headlines set the scene for the prayer petitions that follow, which are said in fairly general language since the details have already been provided.

At a Sunday communion service at Germantown Cumberland Presbyterian Church, worshipers were invited to come to the chancel in two groups of about twenty each and form two concentric circles around the communion table. The persons in the outer circle were given a sheet of paper containing a brief news article, which they were to read aloud while persons in the inner circle were receiving the sacrament. Then the two groups exchanged places and the practice was repeated. The effect was that as communicants were receiving the Eucharist, they were hearing voices around them naming events in the world (good, hopeful events as well as troubling ones). The service was entitled, "Communion in the World." As a less complicated version of this plan, several readers can be stationed around the table reading the news stories continuously as people come and go, eliminating the need to change back and forth between groups.

At a service of Morning Prayer at Memphis Theological Seminary, a world map was printed on the back of the service bulletin. Around the map were printed various world concerns with a line drawn from each to the area on the map to which it applied. Worshipers were asked to voice intercessions in behalf of those places of need throughout the world.

At an All Soul's Day service in 1989 at St. James Episcopal Church in Washington, D.C., fourteen members of the congregation took turns reciting the names of the 373 persons who had been slain in the city since January 1 of that year. It was a solemn litany: the number of homicides was a record high, and nearly two-thirds of them were considered drug-related. After fifteen minutes, the name of victim number 373, Alton Donald Wynne, was read. He had been shot to death only a few hours earlier that day.[40]

These dramatic examples of using contemporary liturgical language would necessitate preparing the worshipers in advance, maybe with a written or verbal commentary given by the worship leader explaining the purpose of the liturgies and providing their theological basis.

---

40. The comments of three persons (*The Washington Post,* 3 November 1989, sec. B, p. 5) attending the service support what we have said above about the effects of using contemporary liturgical language:

"It was sad, very sobering. These are *hard and cold facts.*"

"I think it *helps you take the situation real seriously,* if you haven't already."

"We hope that *God's grace and the power of prayer* will change what's going on." Emphasis added.

The most common way of speaking the language of contemporary events, though, is by including specific petitions, intercessions, and thanksgivings in corporate prayers that arise from current situations. In some cases these will be named before God in a single petition, briefly stated. Here are examples:

- for the people of Poland in their struggle to establish a new government and stabilize their national life.
- for peace in the Middle East.
- for the innocent victims of the drug wars in our city.
- for those who struggle to overcome the ravages of hurricane Hugo.
- for the work and witness of the church in Two-Thirds World countries.
- give strength to our brother, Desmond Tutu, in his fight to win the freedom of his people in South Africa.
- for our sisters and brothers in the San Francisco Bay area as they work to recover from the devastation of an earthquake.
- for the beleaguered people of Haiti.

At other times the petitions will be stated in longer sentences with language more descriptive of the situation. For example:

- for the old man who leans against the wall on Connecticut Avenue every day, holding out a paper cup for spare change; and for the woman who sleeps on the ground at Market Place Square, clutching tightly her two bags of belongings; help us to know how best to minister to these and to all "the least of these," our brothers and sisters.
- for the children at Fletcher-Johnson School in Marshal Heights, who try desperately to keep studying while the popping sounds of gunfire go on outside all around them.
- guide us all as we prepare to go to voting booths next Tuesday, that we may cast our votes not merely from self-interest but from a concern for the public good.
- we give thanks, O God, for the United Nations peace-keeping team being sent to Central America in order to prevent the foreign infiltration of sovereign boundaries; uphold them in their mission, that all fighting may stop, free elections be held, and a just peace be established in that bleeding land.
- we thank you for the daily vigil of the man named Song, who, year after year in Lafayette Square, faithfully bears his witness for disarmament and peace in the world.

Here are some of the intercessions voiced at Holy Name Cathedral in Chicago on 24 March 1990, the tenth anniversary of Oscar Romero's death:

Let us pray for God's peace in El Salvador and throughout the world:
Raise Monseñor Romero's spirit in the hearts of Salvadorans and all who thirst for justice.
Turn all nations from militarism and disrespect for human rights toward a dialogue and national reconciliation.
Peace to El Salvador, peace to South Africa and the Middle East, peace to Lithuania.

Let us pray for those suffering most from injustice:
Sustain the oppressed with a hope like Mary's.
Guard the children and elderly displaced by warring and greed.
Teach us to carry their hopes in our bodies.

Let us pray for those martyred for justice:
Hold the nameless, persecuted thousands forever.
Bless Maureen Courtney and her Sister, the six Jesuits and their associates, Maura Clark, Ita Ford, Dorothy Kazel, and Jean Donovan.
Glorify them.[41]

Some object that when liturgical prayers include petitions worded by the person leading the prayers, the careful and correct language of classic prayerbooks is lost and the liturgy as a whole suffers.[42] It is true that prayers composed by parish clergypersons and lay leaders of worship seldom equal the refined wording of ancient prayers handed down through the ages. It is also granted that, because all liturgical prayers are a part of ritual, they require ritualized language. How we address God in corporate prayer clearly has limits. Few of us would want to return to some of the pop liturgies of the 1960s spoken in artless street language, as in prayers that began, "Hey there, God, it's me again."

However, exclusive use of any prayerbook locks the contemporary church into a culture removed from its own. We have been arguing that the use of any time-bound liturgical language disengages the church's worship from its contemporary public life, and that being the case, it adversely affects the church's nature to be the body of

41. Timothy Fitzgerald, "General Intercessions," Liturgy 90 21 (May/June 1990): 12.
42. For example, see Richard Toporoski, "The Language of Worship," Worship 52 (November 1978): 489–508, and Craig Douglas Erickson, Participating in Worship: History, Theory, and Practice (Louisville: Westminster/John Knox, 1989), 56–58.

Christ in and for the world. Timeless language is not always timely. If the church has been asked to "sing to the Lord a new song," surely it is also asked to "pray to the Lord a new prayer." Jesus himself taught his followers to use a new address for God (no doubt to the consternation of the traditionalists): "abba"—the contemporary (Aramaic), everyday word for "father." Although ritual in the church should be artistic, it is never wholly art—at least aesthetic standards are not the preeminent interest. So, although it is true that the classic prayers of Christian antiquity help to connect today's church with its heritage and contribute richly to the liturgical prayer life of a congregation, they alone cannot fully voice before God a particular congregation's concerns in its own discrete social context. "There is something incongruous about a hardbound collection of intercessions, when these prayers need to be written 'in the field.' We might borrow others' words or images, but we cannot borrow others' prayers."[43]

Yet, contemporary prayer intercessions must be composed with much sensitivity and thought. David Buttrick argues that liturgical language is both public language—the language of the people—and extraordinary language: "Liturgy uses ordinary language in an extraordinary way and, in doing so, stretches language, elevates language, producing a certain oddness."[44] Nowhere is it written as law that contemporary prayers should be "from the top of the head" (which, unfortunately, is sometimes equated with "from the heart"); rather, they should be carefully worded and phrased so that their language is neither too public nor too extraordinary. There is no reason to think the Holy Spirit works only or best in impromptu situations—indeed, it may be that the Spirit works most effectively in persons as they struggle to prepare the prayers to be offered later in the assembly. Justin Martyr instructs the leader of worship to offer "prayers and thanksgivings to the best of his ability"[45]—which supports free prayer but also the discipline that goes with it.

Persons who write prayers for worship need not assume they must work *ex nihilo* (out of nothing). Classic prayers and prayerbooks may

---

43. Timothy Fitzgerald, "General Intercessions—Continued," *Liturgy 90* 21 (July 1990): 15.

44. David G. Buttrick, "On Liturgical Language," *Reformed Liturgy and Music* 15 (Winter 1991): 79.

45. Thomas B. Falls, "The First Apology," *Saint Justin Martyr* in *Fathers of the Church* (New York: Christian Heritage, Inc., 1948), 107.

serve as models; they may be, as James F. White suggests, "our best school of prayer."[46] Suggestions and guidelines for composing prayers for liturgical use are available (see the following section and "Composing and Leading Corporate Prayers" in the Selected Resources at the end of this book). Published collections of contemporary prayers can be used as resources (see "Contemporary Prayers"). Even prayers that have become dated (which, after all, is the inevitable fate of truly contemporary prayers) can be updated, sometimes by substituting names and places or altering the original situation to accommodate a new one.

Liturgical leaders who regularly depend on prayerbooks for their liturgical prayers can contemporize the traditional intercessions by adding a phrase that names a current instance exemplifying the petition, using the word *especially,* to introduce the new phrase.

- ["behold and visit, we pray, the cities of the earth,"] especially our own city, Washington, D.C., in its battle against the scourge of drugs and drug violence.

- ["we remember before you those who suffer want and anxiety from lack of work;"] especially the mine workers on strike at the Pittston coal mines in West Virginia, and the Russian mine workers on strike at the Gorki mines in the Soviet Union.

- ["for all who suffer; for refugees, prisoners, and all who are in danger;"] especially for the eighteen United States hostages who are being held captive in Lebanon.

- ["for the sick and the suffering,"] especially for those who are suffering from the AIDS virus.

- ["for the poor and oppressed, for the unemployed and the destitute;"] especially for migrant workers in the strawberry fields of Louisiana and for cane cutters in Florida.

It would be good if the prayer petitions for Sunday liturgies could be composed by a group made up of the parish clergy and laity—to allow for group discussion of the selection of subjects and the wording of petitions—but constraints of time and schedules seldom allow it. Generally, the minister or lay leader is assigned the responsibility of choosing the relevant matters to be included and of composing the prayers. This is a challenging undertaking, to be sure, yet praying in the language of one's contemporary public is an undertaking full of promise. Intercessions relevant to conditions in today's troubled world

46. White, "Eucharistic Prayer," 21.

represent, like sermons, a vital and lively way for the church's worship to act out the church's commission to be the body of Christ in history. Still, persons who lead corporate prayers will remain sensitive to the fact that such prayers, again, like sermons, deserve and demand language that is appropriate for the address of God. Whenever even their best efforts fail to reach that high goal, they can be assured that the Holy Spirit will intercede for them "with sighs too deep for words" (Rom. 8:26).

Guidelines for Composing Original Prayers[47]

Function and Structure

1. The author should keep in mind the function of the prayer, its place and purpose in the rite.

2. The prayers are intended for *proclamation* in the liturgical assembly.[48]

3. While the traditional elements of a particular genre of prayer should be contained in the newly composed prayers (for example, the classic structure of a collect contains address, amplification of address, petition, result clause, conclusion), they need not in every instance follow exactly the structure of the prayers now in the Sacramentary[49] or other ritual books.

4. The thoughts expressed in the prayers should have a logical coherence and unity and the prayers should have a coherent structure.

5. The nature of the rite as well as the moment in the rite and its ritual context will influence the tone of the prayer.

Content and Style

6. The prayers must be doctrinally sound.

---

47. Original Texts Subcommittee of the International Commission on English in the Liturgy, 1275 K Street, NW, Suite 1202, Washington, DC 20005. These guidelines have been developed over some years and are still being revised and supplemented as a result of the actual experience of developing new prayers for the liturgy. Used by permission of ICEL.

For a helpful discussion and explanation of each of these guidelines, see H. Kathleen Hughes, "Original Texts: Beginnings, Present Projects, Guidelines," in Peter C. Finn and James M. Schellman, eds., *Shaping English Liturgy: Studies in Honor of Archbishop Denis Hurley* (Washington, D.C.: Pastoral Press, 1990), 242–55.

48. That is, they are to be offered in the "public voice" of leading worship, not as if they were the private prayers of the one praying.

49. A book of prayer and ritual of the Catholic Church.

7. Inspiration for the prayers will be found in the Scriptures, the seasons, and the theology underlying the various rites. For example, references to baptism would be expected in some presidential[50] prayers in Lent and the Easter season.

8. The prayers should have enough substance to draw the congregation into prayer and to afford inspiration for meditation.

9. The themes of the prayers should be fairly universal so that they can be used in a variety of places and circumstances. In addition, these compositions are prepared for an international community and should avoid themes that might be suitable for a particular community or region but would be meaningless or confusing in other circumstances.[51]

10. As far as possible the author should avoid moving from the concrete to the abstract. A concrete prayer is one that is rooted in human experience and speaks of basic human concerns. Thus rooted in human experience, a prayer can be concrete and universal at the same time.

11. The compositions should be clear, forceful, interesting, consistent, and imaginative.

12. There should be a consistency of images, and care must be exercised not to use too many images in a single prayer, lest the hearers become confused.

13. An effort should be made to open the prayers to a wide-ranging vocabulary. Color and poetic imagery, where possible, should be evidenced in the compositions. At the same time jargon or esoteric words should be avoided.

14. The prayers should use inclusive language and avoid the use of language that may discriminate on sexist, racist, clericalist, or antisemitic grounds.

15. Attention to rhythm and cadence must be a primary consideration in the composition of new prayers.

16. Attention must be given to the sense lines in the prayers, with a view to their being proclaimed well, heard, and easily understood.

17. Authors should avoid stock-in-trade collect phrases.[52]

---

50. That is, prayers led by the "president," or presider; the person who leads the service.

51. This guideline applies particularly to prayers offered in ecumenical and cross-cultural gatherings.

52. For example, "beseech," "vouchsafe," "exceedingly," "most heartily," "forasmuch as," "wherefore."

18. Original texts should in general be fuller than the corresponding ICEL translations.[53]

Trinitarian Concerns

19. Christian liturgical prayer is traditionally directed to the Father, through the mediation of the Son, in the power of the Spirit.

20. Care must be taken to respect the Trinitarian economy; for example, the Father is not "Truth," the Son is not the "Comforter," and so on.

21. Within the prayers, references to the different persons of the Trinity must be clear, especially when pronouns (like you and he) are being used.

22. Presidential prayers should be addressed to the First Person of the Trinity. Authors are encouraged to incorporate a wide range of metaphors, especially those drawn from the Scriptures, in the forms of address of the prayers. The choice of address should be made bearing in mind the content of the balance of the prayer.

23. While presidential prayers are traditionally addressed to the First Person of the Trinity, there are other genre (for example, litanies) that may be addressed to the Son or the Spirit.

24. Attention must be given to the conclusions of the prayers in order that they express the mediation of Christ. Whether standard or more inventive, the conclusion should fit together with what has gone before in the body of the prayers or it may be interwoven within the prayer. If there is a doxology in the body of the prayer, it seems best to omit a full doxology in the conclusion.

Focused Hymns

When Isaac Watts was sixteen years old, he complained to his father that the hymns being sung in their church, the Above Bar Congregational Church, Southampton, England, were dull and dated; at that time (the seventeenth century) only the Psalms were sung in worship. Watts's father, a deacon in the church, answered, "Then write something better." Young Isaac sat down to write the first of his more than 700 hymns.[54]

---

53. That is, fuller than the brief prayers in the Roman rite.

54. Selma Bishop, *Isaac Watts: Hymns and Spiritual Songs* (London: Faith Press, 1962), xix.

Ever since the day of Watts, succeeding generations of hymnwriters have been encouraging the church to "sing a new song to the Lord"—from the Wesley brothers, to John Mason Neale, to Fanny Crosby, to Erik Routley, down to present-day hymnwriters such as Frederick Kaan, Fred Pratt Green, Jane Parker Huber, Thomas Troeger, Christopher Webber, and Brian Wren. At the same time, though, worshiping congregations have not always welcomed new hymns with enthusiasm or introduced them regularly into their liturgies, preferring instead, like Watts's home congregation, the hymns of times gone by. Still, the more popular hymns being sung in the church today generally reflect an older and a different culture, many of them written in male-dominant language and with the archaisms of Tudor English.[55] In addition, many of the older hymns tend to encourage individualism and subjectivism, with their abundant use of first-person pronouns ("I Need Thee Every Hour," "I Come to the Garden Alone," "O for a Heart to Praise My God") and their focus on the interior life ("Breathe on Me, Breath of God," "Amazing Grace, How Sweet the Sound," "Come, Thou Fount of Every Blessing"). It is true that some older hymns do still carry a contemporary ring, especially hymns from the Social Gospel movement of the nineteenth century. For example, in "The Voice of God Is Calling" there are the lines,

> I hear my people crying
> in slum and mine and mill;
> no field or mart is silent,
> no city street is still

and in "Where Cross the Crowded Ways of Life" there is the stanza

> In haunts of wretchedness and need,
> On shadowed thresholds dark with fears,
> From paths where hide the lures of greed,
> We catch the vision of your tears.

A church needs to sing in the language of its contemporaneous public. Although it is important to join with the saints of the ages in singing the traditional hymns of the church, congregations also need

---

55. Archaic words in the older hymns put us back into an unfamiliar culture. Brian Wren (*Faith Looking Forward* [Carol Stream, Ill.: Hope Publishing Company, 1983], Notes) gives examples: "bosom, bower, dower, affords (meaning 'gives'), mortal, sacred, abide, abode, blessed, bounteous, toil." Other words, such as "oft," "nigh," "follies," "enrapt," and "naught" (the list goes on) do as well.

to seek out and sing the hymns of their own generation. Thankfully, there are several contemporary Isaac Wattses in the church of today whose "new songs to the Lord" are finding their way into worship liturgies. Although it is not possible for the language of these hymns to be as current as the day's newspaper (or, for that matter, the liturgy's sermon and prayers), most of them do voice the modern idiom and today's public conditions far better than most traditional hymnody. What they offer today's church are fresh images and metaphors, words and phrases that reflect the realities of the historical present. A hymn by Brian Wren, the British poet and hymnwriter, contains no less than ten new titles for God: Beautiful Movement, Marker of Rainbows, Spinner of Chaos, Weaver of Stories, Nudging Discomforter, Straight-Talking Lover, Midwife of Changes, Mother of Wisdom, Dare-devil Gambler, and Life-giving Loser.[56]

In a survey of eight new hymnals, David McCormick has found more than 900 new hymn texts written since 1950.[57] At least 425 of these appear in only one of the hymnbooks, yet a number of the new hymns have found a widespread acceptability across various denominational lines. The more popular new hymns include these:

"When in Our Music God Is Glorified," Fred Pratt Green (8)
"Christ upon the Mountain Peak," Brian Wren (7)
"I Come with Joy to Meet My Lord," Brian Wren (7)
"For the Fruit of All Creation," Fred Pratt Green (7)
"Christ Is Alive," Brian Wren (6)
"We Know that Christ Is Raised and Dies No More," John B. Geyer (6)
"Tell Out, My Soul, the Greatness of the Lord," Timothy
   Dudley-Smith (6)
"Earth and All Stars," Herbert Brokering (6)
"God, Who Stretched the Spangled Heavens," Catherine A. Cameron (6)
"All Who Love and Serve Your City," Erik Routley (6)
"There's a Spirit in the Air," Brian Wren (5)
"Jesu, Jesu, Fill Us with Your Love," Tom Colvin (5)
"God Is Here!," Fred Pratt Green (5)

56. Brian Wren, *What Language Shall I Borrow? God-Talk in Worship: A Male Response to Feminist Theology* (New York: Crossroad, 1989), 140. See also Thomas Troeger's hymn "Source and Sovereign, Rock and Cloud," which contains thirty-nine names or titles for God (*The United Methodist Hymnal* [Nashville: United Methodist Publishing House, 1989], 113).

57. David W. McCormick, "What's New in the New Hymnals?" *Liturgy* 9 (Fall 1990): 61.

"Lord, You Give the Great Commission," Jeffery Rowthorn (5)
"New Songs of Celebration Render," Erik Routley (5)[58]

Four of the most recent Protestant hymnals, *Rejoice in the Lord: A Hymn Companion to the Scriptures*,[59] *The Presbyterian Hymnal: Hymns, Psalms, and Spiritual Songs*,[60] *The United Methodist Hymnal*,[61] and *Psalter Hymnal*,[62] while retaining many of the familiar ancient hymns and gospel songs of the church, have added a substantial number of the new hymns. Discussions of the relative merits of the hymnals can be found elsewhere; our purpose is to point out the repertory of new texts included in the new hymnbooks.[63]

Rejoice in the Lord includes 85 new hymns by hymnwriters such as Fred Pratt Green (14), Brian Wren (9), Erik Routley (8), and F. Bland Tucker (8). The new Presbyterian hymnal contains 215 new hymns by such hymnwriters as Fred Anderson (15), Fred Pratt Green (15), Jane Parker Huber (11), Brian Wren (11), Fred Kaan (10), Christopher Webber (9), and Thomas Troeger (8). The United Methodist hymnal contains 168 contemporary hymns by writers such as Fred Pratt Green (16), Brian Wren (14), Fred Kaan (6), Jacques Berthier (5), and Skinner Chávez-Melo (5). The *Psalter Hymnal*, the hymnbook of the Christian Reformed Church, contains 109 new hymns by writers such as Marie J. Post (11), Calvin Seerveld (9), Brian Wren (4), Christopher Idle (4), and Fred Pratt Green (3).

A new nondenominational hymnal, *The Worshiping Church*,[64] also

58. McCormick, "What's New," 63–67. The number in parentheses indicates the number of hymnals that include the hymn.

59. Erik Routley, ed., *Rejoice in the Lord: A Hymn Companion to the Scriptures* (Grand Rapids, Mich.: Wm. B. Eerdmans, 1985). For a review of this hymnal, see William P. Rowan, *The Hymn: A Journal of Congregational Song* 37 (April 1986): 45–46, and Robert Stigall, *Reformed Liturgy and Music* 20 (Summer 1986): 121–22.

60. *The Presbyterian Hymnal: Hymns, Psalms, and Spiritual Songs* (Louisville: Westminster/John Knox, 1990). For a review of this hymnal, see Fred R. Anderson, "Three New Voices," *Theology Today* 68 (October 1990): 260–72.

61. *Methodist Hymnal*. For a critique of this hymnal, see Carol Doran and Thomas H. Troeger, "The United Methodist Hymnal," *Worship* 65 (March 1991): 159–69.

62. *Psalter Hymnal* (Grand Rapids, Mich.: Christian Reformed Church, 1987). For a review of this hymnal, see Morgan Simmons, " 'Psalter Hymnal'—A Review," *The Hymn: A Journal of Congregational Song* 40 (October 1989): 16–18.

63. For this survey, hymns by living hymnwriters and hymns written since 1960 by hymnwriters recently deceased have been included. New tunes, arrangements, paraphrases, responses, and short choruses have not been counted.

64. *The Worshiping Church: A Hymnal* (Carol Stream, Ill.: Hope Publishing Company, 1990).

contains considerable contemporary hymnody—the publisher, Hope Publishing Company, is one of the leading publishers of contemporary church music. The hymnal includes an impressive 245 new hymns and songs, a substantial amount of which is of the "praise song" variety. Representative hymnwriters are Timothy Dudley-Smith (19), Fred Pratt Green (17), Christopher Martin Idle (15), Bryan Jeffery Leech (13), Margaret Clarkson (12), and Brian Wren (8).

Among the new Catholic hymnals, *Worship III*[65] contains a basic repertory of modern hymns by Fred Pratt Green (12), Timothy Dudley-Smith (12), David Hurd (9), Brian Wren (9), and Fred Kaan (8). Its companion volume, *Gather*,[66] is a collection of songs of the folk variety garnered from numerous writers such as Marty Haugen (43), David Hass (34), Michael Joncas (18), and Jacques Berthier of the Taizé Community (20).[67] Another recent Catholic hymnal, *Lead Me, Guide Me, The Hymnal for African American Catholics*,[68] contains some contemporary hymnody—mostly "praise" and folk songs—but, because the hymnal contains no index of authors and the documentation for many hymns omits the date, it is not possible to determine the number of contemporary songs in the hymnal.

The new hymnals' topical indexes provide evidence of their intent to connect the church's singing with the church's ministry to today's world. They include such topic headings as:

Aging/Old Age	Liberation
Anxiety	Poverty
Church in the World	Prisoners
City/Urban Life	Prosperity
Cosmos	Race and Culture
Ecology/Environment	Science
Ecumenism	Society/Social Concerns
Hunger, Physical	Stress
Industry and Labor	War/Conflict
Justice	World Peace
Leisure	

---

65. *Worship*, 3rd ed. (Chicago: G.I.A. Publications, Inc., 1986).

66. *Gather* (Chicago: G.I.A. Publications, Inc., 1988).

67. For a review of these hymnals, see George Black, "*Gather* and *Worship:* One Concept in Two Books and Many Editions," *The Hymn* 42 (April 1991): 12–15.

68. *Lead Me, Guide Me* (Chicago: G.I.A. Publications, Inc., 1987). For a review of this hymnal, see William Farley Smith, "Lead Me, Guide Me: The African American Catholic Hymnal," *The Hymn* 40 (January 1989): 13–15.

The new hymnal for Southern Baptist congregations, *The Baptist Hymnal*,[69] contains nearly 150 new texts. Multiple hymns are included by Timothy Dudley-Smith (7), Fred Pratt Green (7), Bryan Jeffery Leech (5), and Brian Wren (5), but the majority of the new texts are single works by one writer. For the most part, these hymns are new only in a chronological sense: their language and imagery are strongly biblical, often a paraphrase of Scripture or even a literal quotation, and the traditional religious interests of the hymns make few connections with contemporary social situations.

Nothing like a thorough description of the new hymnals can be given here, or even a decent sampling; it will have to be enough to say that these hymnals are providing the church with hymns in a language and with images that engage the worshiping people of God with life-situations of their own generation. For example, Herbert Brokering's stirring hymn "Earth and All Stars" includes, along with the more traditional sources of divine praise—planets, flowers, trumpet, and pipes—these modern sources:

> Engines and steel! Come, pounding hammers!
> Sing to the Lord a new song!
> Limestone and beams! Strong building workers!
> Sing to the Lord a new song!
> Classrooms and labs! Come, boiling test tubes!
> Sing to the Lord a new song!
> Athlete and band! Loud cheering people!
> Sing to the Lord a new song![70]

Many contemporary hymnwriters are sensitive to social and environmental issues that are acutely relevant to life in today's world. Ecology, peace and justice, urban problems, and human suffering are subjects that often find their way into contemporary hymnody. For example, "O Lord, You Gave Your Servant John," by Joy F. Patterson:

> Our cities, Lord, wear shrouds of pain;
> Beneath our gleaming towers of wealth
> The homeless crouch in rain and snow,
> The poor cry out for strength and health.
> Youth's hope is dimmed by ignorance;

69. *The Baptist Hymnal* (Nashville: Convention Press, 1991).
70. *Psalter Hymnal*, 433.

Unwilling, workers idled stand;
Indifference walks unheeding by
As hunger stretches out its hand.

Come, Lord, make real John's vision fair;
Come, dwell with us, make all things new;
We try in vain to save our world
Unless our help shall come from You.
Come, strengthen us to live in love;
Bid hatred, greed, injustice cease.
Your glory all the light we need,
Let all our cities shine forth peace.[71]

Another example is this hymn, "For the Healing of the Nations," by
Fred Kaan:

For the healing of the nations, Lord we pray with one accord;
for a just and equal sharing of the things that earth affords;
to a life of love in action help us rise and pledge our word.

All that kills abundant living, let it from the earth be banned;
pride of status, race, or schooling, dogmas that obscure your plan.
In our common quest for justice may we hallow life's brief span.[72]

Fred Pratt Green's hymn "When Our Confidence Is Shaken" addresses the problem of pervasive skepticism in our age, both inside
and outside the church.

When our confidence is shaken in beliefs we thought secure,
when the spirit in its sickness seeks but cannot find a cure,
God is active in the tensions of a faith not yet mature.

Solar systems, void of meaning, freeze the spirit into stone;
always our researches lead us to the ultimate unknown.
Faith must die, or come full circle to its source in God alone.

In the discipline of praying, when it's hardest to believe;
in the drudgery of caring, when it's not enough to grieve;
faith, maturing, learns acceptance of the insights we receive.

God is love, and thus redeems us in the Christ we crucify;
this is God's eternal answer to the world's eternal why.
May we in this faith maturing be content to live and die![73]

---

71. *The Presbyterian Hymnal* (Louisville: Westminster/John Knox, 1990), 431.
72. *Gather,* 643, and other hymnals.
73. *Methodist Hymnal,* 505.

Thomas Troeger's hymns are usually closely linked with specific biblical texts; yet the language and imagery of the hymns gives the biblical account a strikingly modern sound. For example, this one is based on Mark 1:23-28:

> "Silence! frenzied, unclean spirit,"
> Cried God's healing, Holy One.
> "Cease your ranting! Flesh can't bear it.
> Flee as night before the sun."
> At Christ's voice the demon trembled,
> From its victim madly rushed,
> While the crowd that was assembled
> Stood in wonder, stunned and hushed.[74]

Most hymnbooks contain only a limited number of hymns specifically written for children and youth, but some of them reflect the realities of youthful life: living with nature, getting along with each other at home and school, playing and sharing and eating together. For example, this song of thanks by Caryl Micklem in Erik Routley's great work, *Rejoice in the Lord*:

> Father, we thank you for the light that shines all the day:
> for human skill's exploration of your creation,
> Father, we thank you.
> Father, we thank you for the friends that brighten our way:
> for your command to call others sisters and brothers,
> Father, we thank you.[75]

Not all new church hymnody is written in traditional styles. For example, folk songs, choruses, and the simple melodies of the Taizé Community are finding their way into congregational singing and, indeed, are often the kind of new music most readily accepted. Another musical genre, rising in popularity, is the music associated with the "praise and worship" style of worship—worship that emphasizes prayer, communal intimacy, emotion, and spontaneous physical movement, and that begins with a period set aside for praise, only

74. Carol Doran and Thomas Troeger, *New Hymns for the Lectionary: To Glorify the Maker's Name* (New York: Oxford University Press, 1986), 52, and in numerous hymnals.

75. Erik Routley, *Rejoice in the Lord* (Grand Rapids, Mich.: Wm. B. Eerdmans, 1985), 16.

after which the worship period proceeds.[76] The songs tend to reflect the style of worship: they are simple, often repetitive, in the traditional language of the Bible (often paraphrased), and are frequently accompanied by hand-clapping and a variety of musical instruments. Originally, the songs were collected independently, but a number of the songs now appear in some of the recent denominational hymnals. Of the 25 most popular "praise and worship" songs, the following appear in the newer mainstream church hymnals:[77]

"Majesty," Jack Hayford (UM, WC, B)
"I Love You, Lord," Laurie Klein (WC, B)
"Praise the Name of Jesus," Roy Hicks, Jr. (WC)
"Jesus, Name Above All Names," Naida Hern (WC)
"This Is the Day," Les Garrett (UM, WC, B, PsH)
"Glorify Thy Name," Donna Adkins (WC, B, PsH)
"Our God Reigns," Leonard Smith (PsH)
"Give Thanks," Henry Smith (WC)
"Thou Art Worthy," Pauline Mills (WC, PsH)
"Bless His Holy Name," Andrae Crouch (WC, B, PsH)
"Open Our Eyes, Lord," Bob Cull (WC, B)
"We Have Come into His House," Bruce Ballinger (B)
"Seek Ye First," Karen Lafferty (UM, WC, B, PsH, Pr, W)
"How Majestic Is Your Name," Michael W. Smith (WC, B)
"His Name Is Wonderful," Audrey Mieir (UM, WC, B)
"Bind Us Together," Bob Gillman (WC)
"Emmanuel," Bob McGee (UM, WC, B)
"O, How He Loves You and Me," Kurt Kaiser (WC, B)
Totals: WC = 16, B = 11, PsH = 6, UM = 5, Pr = 1, W = 1.

Admittedly, not all new church music is of the highest quality. Music of the "pop" variety, what some critics term "Jesus-jingles," is gaining wide appeal in some segments of the church. Much of what is called "Christian rock" and "contemporary gospel" music is a spin-off from popular secular music and is of dubious quality, if not an abomination to the Lord. As a rule it is contemporary neither in language nor context, but merely sets traditional religious language and images to popular, often sentimental, musical styles.

76. See Robert Webber, "Enter His Courts with Praise," *Reformed Worship* 20 (June 1991), 9. The entire issue focuses on the "Praise and Worship" movement.
77. Bert Polman, "The Praise and Worship Hit Parade," *Reformed Worship* 20 (July 1991): 33. Abbreviations used: *United Methodist* (UM), *Worshiping Church* (WC), *Baptist* (B), *Psalter Hymnal* (PsH), *Presbyterian* (Pr), *Worship* (W).

However, today's churches would do well to consider that being an inclusive congregation requires a considerable tolerance of varying musical tastes. Music purists may equate a tolerance of taste with a compromise of quality, yet a mutual respect for different cultural expressions lies at the center of any heterogeneous Christian community. C. S. Lewis put it this way: "For the sake of love, the worshipper of high musical taste should put up with poor quality, and the worshipper of low taste with highbrow stuff."[78]

All liturgy depends on congregational consensus. So, for example, the publication of *Worship III* and *Gather* as companion volumes represents the realistic realization that broad tastes crossing several musical genres exist in most congregations. One might wonder whether the new Presbyterian hymnal represents an instance of setting the musical and theological standards for its hymnody too high by excluding so many well-known hymns and gospel songs from its repertory. However, it could be argued that the new United Methodist hymnal errs on the side of compromise by including so many traditional songs and hymns of dubious quality—yet there can be no argument that this hymnal reaches a wider range of musical tastes. Taste in music is notoriously difficult to define and preferences vary among church bodies. Parish worship leaders and church music committees will need to evaluate the relative quality of the new church music to determine its suitability for the liturgies of their congregations.

Overall, the present is an exciting time for church music.[79] Today's church is no longer limited by necessity to a repertory of hymns from other times and settings but has music available that is in the contemporary idiom and connected to the life events of its own time. The classic hymns need not be either disregarded or replaced; the traditional does not die out, it is expanded. Some day, perhaps, "Lord, You Give the Great Commission" will become the church's "Onward Christian Soldiers" in popularity, and "Christ Is Alive! Let Christians Sing" will become another "Christ the Lord Is Risen Today"—after which they, too, in time, will be supplemented with newer hymns.

---

78. An indirect citation in Jock Stein, *Singing a New Song: Fresh Resources for Christian Praise* (Edinburgh: Hansel Press, 1988), 6.

79. For an evaluation of contemporary church music and a projection of its future, see Virgil C. Funk, ed., *Sung Liturgy: Toward 2000 A.D.* (Washington, D.C.: Pastoral Press, 1991).

In sermon, prayer, and song, the voice of the present-day church can be a "new utterance" reflecting the time and events in which the church exists. The liturgical language of the church in every generation will share the language of its contemporaneous public because the church exists in and for that public. The church is not asked to abandon its liturgical traditions; indeed, it must remain linked with its biblical and theological heritage. But the church is asked to incorporate into its received liturgies new liturgical expressions that open up the worship of God to the concerns and conditions of the historical present. That this represents an ongoing need for liturgical change is obvious; but the new liturgical resources being provided by major denominations are evidence that a significant segment of the church is free enough and willing enough to participate in these changes.

To adapt the traditional language of Christian worship to present historical realities is only to continue in and by the Spirit of Pentecost, who empowers the church to speak with the "new utterance" that engages the church with its culture. This stanza from Thomas Troeger's hymn voices the church's ongoing prayer:

Holy Spirit, wind and flame, move within our mortal frame;
make our hearts an altar pyre; kindle them with your own fire.
Breathe and blow upon that blaze till our lives, our deeds, and ways
speak that tongue which every land by your grace shall understand.[80]

80. *Methodist Hymnal*, 538.

4

Including
All Persons

Carl Sandburg, the poet, writer, and wordsmith, was once asked by a reporter, "What in your opinion is the ugliest word in the English language?" He thought awhile, then answered, growling it out as if it tasted bad in his mouth: "Exclusive!" If Sandburg is right, and much empirical data is unquestionably on his side, then we could ask, "What is the most beautiful word in the English language?" and expect the opposite answer: "Inclusive!"

Historically, the Christian church has regarded the word *inclusive* as one of the most beautiful words of its faith. The Christian biblical and theological understanding of humankind is that all persons are a part of the human family; each person is equally loved, judged, and valued by God. Acts of prejudice against any person, no matter their color or creed or national origin, are considered sins against God. Again and again, the Jesus of the Gospels shocked and infuriated the social traditionalists of his day by treating women as his equals, associating with social pariahs, and socializing with the infamous. In the early church, Paul's affirmation that "there is neither Jew nor Greek, there is neither slave nor free, there is neither male nor female; for you are all one in Christ Jesus" (Gal. 3:29) was understood to be the rule of practice, not exception. All instances of racism, nationalism, sexism, and other forms of discrimination that blotch the church's historical record (and they are shamefully many) are aberrations. When the church is true to its nature as the body of Jesus Christ, it is socially inclusive.

Expressing Gender Equality

In what ways might the church's liturgical language reflect its theological nature to be socially inclusive? At its most basic level, the church's worship will carefully screen from its language words and phrases that in any way stereotype or exclude or alienate persons. Not a banality, words that exclude are often subtle, and unless one is intentionally sensitive to the danger, linguistic exclusion will result.

Regrettably, society in general does not seem to be as much aware of the ugliness in the word *exclusive* as Sandburg was—or if it is, it shows a remarkable tolerance of it.[1] Discriminatory speech continues to show up in news reports, political commentary, television sit-coms, locker-room talk, and even polite conversation. Women, people of color, persons who are old, disabled, gay, or who are "different" in almost any discernable way certainly still encounter exclusion. In sports, Native Americans are caricatured as Chiefs, Redskins, or Braves who wave tomahawks and sing war chants. Stereotypical language about persons who are poor, persons who receive welfare checks (the linguistic put-down is "living *off* welfare"), aliens, and, especially since the Persian Gulf war, Arabs, seems to have a tenacious grip on our culture that will not let go.[2] Secular society seems to have "ins" and "outs" for its language as much as for its fashions; it is a language that divests persons of their God-given worth and dignity.

But the language of the church is not the language of secular society. When Christians speak in worship (as well as elsewhere), they speak with the words of Jesus, which are words of healing, not hurt, which dignify persons, not demean them, and which take persons seriously, not patronize them. The language the church speaks in its worship is one point at which the church is uncompromisingly at odds with culture. To the degree it represents its Lord, the church's liturgy stands

1. The headline for a story in today's paper (*The Commercial Appeal,* 9 January 1991, sec. A, p. 2), taken off the *Washington Post* wire, reads: "Whites view minorities negatively, says survey," and begins: "A majority of whites questioned in a national survey believe blacks and Hispanics prefer welfare to work and tend to be lazier than whites, more prone to violence, less intelligent and less patriotic."

2. For example, consider this news item in a daily paper (Chuck Stone, "For Affirmative Action," *The Commercial Appeal,* 5 June 1990, sec. A, p. 7): "On the concert circuit, the most popular comedians, rock groups and rappers are those whose routines dehumanize Asians, blacks, gays, Jews or women. Spewing bilious bigotry on stage, these performers are making hatred legitimate and ethnic antagonism respectable."

over against the destructive discriminatory language of its culture and refuses to speak it.

So worship leaders who write the prayers and sermons and hymns used in worship, and those who make the parish announcements or welcome newcomers, and, yes, those who read the scripture lessons, will give intentional care to the language they speak, so that it reflects the inclusive nature of the reign of God—so that all may be incorporated into the one body of Christ. In this way the church will be at work in the world, by repudiating speech that degrades or excludes classes of people, and by receiving into its worship the very ones who social convention says do not belong.

For example, worship in the Times Square Church that sprang up in an old theatre building off Times Square in New York City was described this way: "This may be the most diverse crowd ever to pray together. Prostitutes, drug addicts, AIDS patients, and the homeless mix with middle- and upper-class singles and families from Manhattan, the suburbs of Connecticut and New Jersey. At most services, well-dressed worshipers outnumber street people 2 to 1, but that doesn't stop everyone in the congregation from exchanging hugs and handshakes of peace."[3]

A reporter describes an AIDS vigil she attended at a Catholic church in San Francisco. From a back pew, she observed elderly, longtime members of the church interact with younger members, many of whom had the AIDS virus. A 70-year-old woman held a young man "emaciated by AIDS" by the belt so he could receive the Eucharist. Another "white-haired, Italian-American woman in thick, black, orthopedic shoes hobbled up the aisles saying 'Peace be with you,' to gay men wearing t-shirts, leather jackets, and business suits."[4]

Both Genders Included

The church's liturgical speech will be inclusive in regard to gender. It is a painful admission to make, but for almost all of its life, the language of the church's liturgies has been rigidly androcentric; that is, references to God, titles and names for God, collective nouns, indefinite pronouns, and other grammatical allusions to gender have been almost

3. *The Commercial Appeal*, 31 December 1988, sec. C, p. 4.
4. Kay Butler, in *Family Therapy Networker*, cited in Bob Hulteen, "Worthy of Note," *Sojourners* 20 (June 1991): 48.

exclusively masculine. The male-dominant language in the church only mirrors the patriarchal social order that has existed almost universally from ancient times, in which the male was the unquestioned head of the family, government, business, and, indeed, of all social institutions. At present, a significant segment of the church is seriously striving to change its speech to become gender-inclusive, not because it is the trendy or politically correct thing to do, or because of pressure from the feminist movement, as is sometimes charged, but because churches are coming at last to acknowledge that androcentric language excludes. The issue is not merely political or practical; it is theological. God's love as seen in Christ levels class and status distinctions, eliminates ranks of subordination. The language the church speaks will reflect that all-encompassing divine love.

We have already noted that language is not value-neutral; the language we use gives away who we are, what we think. We have also noted that words have creative power; words can construct or destruct, they can hurt or heal. Language matters. So, if someone should say, "Whenever I use the word 'man' or 'mankind,' I don't really mean males only, and when I refer to God as 'Him,' I don't really mean that He is male," that person is disregarding the active creative power of language. (It also reminds me of how, in the South of my youth, people used to say, about the way they referred to African Americans, "Oh, I just call them 'nigra' or 'boy'; I don't really mean anything racist by it.") Exclusively male language devalues the influence, even the presence, of women, and renders them subordinate to and dependent upon men. So it follows that male-dominant liturgical language communicates the point of view, even the theological belief, that the church has bestowed a preference and prominence upon its members who are male—which, surely, is the reason that, only until recently, the significant places of leadership in the church, Catholic and Protestant, have been held almost exclusively by men.[5]

5. Hierarchical authority in the church has been patriarchal for most of its life. Notice this Call to Worship taken from a worship liturgy:
    Leader: O God of Abraham, Isaac, and Jacob;
    People: God of Amos, Isaiah, and Jeremiah;
    Leader: God of Jesus and the Apostles;
    People: God of Luther, Calvin, and Wesley;
    Leader: God of McAdow, Ewing, and King; . . .
About twenty-five personal names or allusions are made here; not one of them is a woman (the last three names are of founders of the Cumberland Presbyterian Church).

Further, androcentric language helps shape our view of God. Prevailing linguistic terminology exerts a power of influence over images and concepts. Using exclusively male terms and images for God generates a perception of God with male attributes and acting in characteristically male ways. For example, the person whose titles for God are predominantly sovereign (Judge, King, Creator, Lord, Ruler) will likely perceive God as omnipotent, invulnerable, and transcendent. But what about the "other side" of God—the vulnerable, suffering, meek God?[6] "Our images can set limits to our ability to understand God."[7] The church's liturgical speech needs to include a wide variety of word-pictures of God that expand, not narrow, how its members perceive God.

So the church, or at least a segment of it, is trying to change its liturgical speech in order to become more inclusive of women and to increase feminine images of God. For example, one denominational body has issued this official statement:

> Our liturgical use of language about God needs enrichment. In the recent past only a few biblical images of God have been employed along with an over-dependence upon the masculine pronoun. The Bible offers many more ways to speak about God. We need to make strenuous efforts in incorporating this wide range of imagery. Terms which unmask old stereotypes wait to be used. . . . New hymns, new prayers, new affirmations of faith, and liturgical-creedal elements can be written and should be an order of high priority in view of the fact that language significantly influences the perceptions of those who use it.[8]

Three Levels of Change

Linguistic changes taking place in Christian liturgy can be categorized on three levels—recognizing that in anyone's personal usage, any combination from a number of these levels is a possibility.[9]

6. For discussions on broadening the images and metaphors for God, see Sallie McFague, *Models of God: Theology for an Ecological, Nuclear Age* (Philadelphia: Fortress Press, 1987); Brian Wren, *What Language Shall I Borrow? God-Talk in Worship: A Male Response to Feminist Theology* (New York: Crossroad, 1989); and James W. Fowler, *Weaving the New Creation: Stages of Faith and the Public Church* (San Francisco: Harper San Francisco, 1991).

7. Isabel Wood Rogers, *In a Word: the Power of Language* (Atlanta: Division of National Mission, the General Assembly Mission Board Presbyterian Church [U.S.A.], n.d.), 5.

8. *United Presbyterian Church Minutes* Part I, Journal (New York: Office of the General Assembly, 1975): 528.

9. Numerous books have been published on this subject: Sharon Neufer Emswiler,

The first level is the most conservative one. It represents changes made within traditional language that convey the full and equal partnership of women with men as human:

1. Eliminating most male collective nouns ("mankind" to "humankind" or "all people," "chairman" to "chairperson," "workman" to "worker").

2. Adding the feminine counterpart to certain masculine nouns and pronouns ("brothers *and sisters*," fathers *and mothers*," "Abraham *and Sarah*," "him *or her*," "himself *or herself*").

3. Changing impersonal pronouns from the singular to the plural to avoid using the masculine ("a person doesn't always get his way" to "people don't always get their way") or to the second person ("you don't always get your way").

4. Reversing the traditional order of two-gender phrases ("women and men," "sisters and brothers," "girls and boys").

5. Increasing the frequency of feminine names, personalities, and images (mother, birthing, womb, bosom, midwife, seamstress, queen) in prayers, sermon illustrations, examples, similes, and metaphors.

The next level of change for a more inclusive liturgical language includes the changes of the first level but goes further. At this level, persons use language that attempts to neutralize traditional language so that the patriarchal worldview assumed in traditional language will not be reinforced:

1. Avoiding the use of masculine pronouns for God, where the change is not unduly awkward ("God blesses His people" to "God blesses God's people" or "God's people are blessed," "God's power and His majesty" to "God's power and majesty").

2. Using the title "Father" for God infrequently.

3. Using other traditional gender-neutral terms for God ("Maker," "Creator," "Refuge," Sovereign One," "Our Rock and Strength").

4. Changing masculine collective nouns, pronouns for God, and the like into gender-neutral language in many hymns, songs, prayerbooks,

---

Words and Worship: A Guide to Nonsexist Hymns, Prayers, and Liturgies, rev. ed. (San Francisco: Harper & Row, 1984); Wren, *What Language Shall I Borrow?* and Gail Ramshaw, *Worship: Searching for Language* (Washington, D.C.: Pastoral Press, 1988). For a brief article on the subject, see Laura Mol, "Wrestling with the Living Word," *Sojourners* 19 (May 1990); 23–26. An excellent resource for use with congregations is *Words that Hurt, Words that Heal* (Nashville: Graded Press, 1990); order from The United Methodist Publishing House, P.O. Box 801, Nashville, TN 37202.

and some scripture readings ("Dear Lord and Father of Mankind" to "O Loving God of Humankind," "I appeal to you, brethren" to "I appeal to you, brothers and sisters," "If anyone hears my voice and opens the door, I will eat with him and he with me" to "If those who hear my voice open the door, I will eat with them and they with me").

5. Changing third-person references to God into direct address (in the Magnificat, "The Lord has shown strength with his arm" to "You have shown strength with your arm").[10]

6. Reducing the number of masculine pronouns with reference to Jesus and the Holy Spirit.

A third level of change in the effort to make liturgical language more gender-inclusive is the most far-reaching. All of the changes listed above would probably be practiced in a thoroughgoing way. But this level goes further than the others by including linguistic changes that undertake naming the realities of God and the Christian faith in such a way that the traditional language is denied authority and a new communal consciousness is established:

1. Avoiding the use of masculine nouns and pronouns for God, such as "Father," "King," and "Lord."

2. Occasionally using "Mother," "Mother and Father," or "Parent," as terms for God, and "She" and "Her" as pronouns for God.

3. Substituting gender-neutral titles of Jesus ("the Human One" for "the Son of man," and "Child" for "Son").

4. Substituting gender-neutral titles in the traditional Trinitarian formula ("Father, Son, and Holy Spirit" to "Creator, Redeemer, and Sanctifier," or "Creator, Christ, and Holy Spirit").

5. Eliminating sexist language from almost all materials used in worship liturgies, including scripture readings (by using *Lectionary for the Christian People*[11] and other such liturgical materials), and eliminating from general use liturgical materials that cannot be altered because of copyright laws or phrasing or rhyming difficulties.

---

10. The English Language Liturgical Consultation revises the Benedictus and the Magnificat in this way (cf. *Praying Together* [Nashville: Abingdon Press, 1988], 45, 49).

11. Gordon Lathrop and Gail Ramshaw, *Lectionary for the Christian People* (Minneapolis: Augsburg Fortress, Year A: 1986, Year B: 1987, Year C: 1988). Also see *Inclusive Language Psalms for Years A, B, and C* (New York: Pilgrim Press, 1987) and *An Inclusive-Language Lectionary* (Philadelphia: John Knox Press, Year A: 1983, Year B: 1984, Year C: 1985). Parishioners at St. Stephen and the Incarnation Episcopal Church in Washington, D.C., have written their own inclusive-language lectionary, *Hearing the Word*, following an intensive four-year study. It can be ordered from the church at 1525 Newton Street NW, Washington, DC 20010.

6. Introducing new hymns, prayers, and other resources into the liturgy that reflect new understandings of theological language about God and the Christian faith.

Many of the revised worshipbooks, lectionaries, and general publications of mainstream denominational publishing houses are incorporating the linguistic changes at least on the first level, and some—the United Methodist, the United Church of Christ, Disciples of Christ, Lutheran and Presbyterian bodies, and several Catholic publishers—clearly have introduced changes on the second level as well.

Some of the recently published hymnals have eliminated or altered much gender-specific language with reference to humans contained in earlier editions.[12] For example, in the hymn "Joyful, Joyful, We Adore Thee," the line "brother love binds man to man" now reads "binding all within its span"[13] or "joining all in heaven's plan"[14] or "joining people hand in hand."[15] The hymn "Good Christian Men, Rejoice" is now "Good Christian Friends, Rejoice,"[16] and the line "though the eye of sinful man" in the hymn "Holy, Holy, Holy, Lord God Almighty" has been rendered gender-inclusive in a number of ways.[17]

Among the more recent hymnals, the Presbyterian hymnal has most significantly reduced the masculine terminology with reference to God. For example, in "All Creatures of Our God and King," the line "praise God and on him cast your care" now reads, "praise God and on God cast your care," and the recurring phrase "O praise him" is changed

---

12. See Gracia Grindal, "Inclusive Language in Hymns: A Reappraisal," *Currents in Theology and Mission* 16 (April 1989): 187–93.

13. *The United Methodist Hymnal* (Nashville: United Methodist Publishing House, 1989), 89.

14. *The Presbyterian Hymnal: Hymns, Psalms, and Spiritual Songs* (Louisville: Westminster/John Knox, 1990), 464.

15. *Worship: A Hymnal and Service Book for Roman Catholics,* 3rd ed. (Chicago: G.I.A. Publications, Inc., 1986), 529.

16. *United Methodist Hymnal,* 224; *Presbyterian Hymnal,* 28; *Worship,* 391; *The Worshiping Church: A Hymnal* (Carol Stream, Ill.: Hope Publishing Company, 1990), 157; *Lutheran Book of Worship* (Minneapolis: Augsburg, 1978), 55; *Hymnbook 1982* (New York: The Church Hymnal Corporation, 1982), 107; *Rejoice in the Lord* (Grand Rapids, Mich.: Wm. B. Eerdmans, 1985), 218; and *Psalter Hymnal* (Grand Rapids: CRC Publications, 1988), 355.

17. "Though the eye of sinfulness," *Rejoice,* 611, *Presbyterian Hymnal,* 138; "though the eye of sinful flesh," *Worshiping Church,* 2; "though the eye made blind by sin," *Worship,* 485, *LBW,* 165, and *Psalter Hymnal,* 249; "though the sinful human eye," *Hymnbook 1982,* 362. Astonishingly, *United Methodist Hymnal* retains the original (64).

to "Alleluia."[18] The hymnal includes three modern versions of the twenty-third Psalm that use gender-neutral language for God.[19]

The Difficulty of Changes

Much of the controversy that continues to swirl throughout the church over issues of inclusive language centers in the third level of changes listed above—and, clearly, this is where the more substantial changes occur. Some object that these changes simply "go too far" beyond traditional liturgical expressions; they overwhelm the familiarity of the church's traditional language and images of deity with strange and unfamiliar forms. Does what is gained by the changes, they ask, compensate for what is lost?[20]

Other persons are concerned about altering the original biblical texts (that is, extant texts, since no original texts exist). They may not be troubled by substituting "men and women" for "men" or "brothers and sisters" for "brothers" in the Greek text because both men and women were clearly meant in the original text. They wonder if changing, for example, the "Son of Man" title for Jesus to "the Human One" introduces theological dimensions to the person of Jesus that are not implied in the original title.

Ethical questions also emerge. Removing sexist language from the traditional hymns of the church does express the church's intention to be linguistically inclusive, but do we have the right, ethically, to alter the original hymnwriter's work?

Still other persons wrestle with theological questions. Eliminating the term *Lord* effectively removes the masculine reference, but it also eliminates the fundamental biblical understanding of the hierarchical relationship between God and humanity. (On the other hand, some changes can improve the theological content of terms: changing "kingdom of God" to "reign of God" retains the concept of God's sovereignty while removing the anachronistic idea of "kingdom").

The question of altering the Trinitarian formula into inclusive terminology is a particularly thorny theological issue. Referring to the

18. *Presbyterian Hymnal,* 455. The *United Methodist Hymnal* changes the line to "O praise ye" but retains the gender adjectives for aspects of nature: "brother sun," "sister moon," "brother fire," and "our sister, gentle death" (62).

19. *Presbyterian Hymnal,* 173, 174, 175.

20. For example, see Louis Roy, "Inclusive Language Regarding God," *Worship* 65 (May 1991): 207–15.

Trinity as "Creator, Redeemer, and Sanctifier" carries different theological content than "Father, Son, and Holy Spirit." Gail Ramshaw has offered an alternative version of the Doxology, to complement (not replace) the familiar version:

Praise God, the Abba bearing love;
Praise God, the Servant from above;
Praise God, the Paraclete we share;
O triune God, receive our prayer.[21]

But in this version "Abba" is the Aramaic word for "Father," so it is gender-neutral only if its meaning is not known, and "Paraclete" is an obscure and odd-sounding term for the Holy Spirit (and carries liturgical problems—it is only one sound removed from "parakeet"). Ruth Duck contends that there is no real need to preserve the triadic form of the traditional formula. She says, " 'I baptize you in the name of God who has been made known through [or, embodied in] Jesus Christ' makes a stronger christological statement than 'I baptize you in the name of Creator, Redeemer, and Sustainer.' "[22]

Obviously, determining precisely how to speak in inclusive ways in worship is no simple matter. Changes some persons regard as crucial, others regard as nit-picking. Gail Ramshaw says that when making decisions about inclusive language, "one feels like the city council deciding on curbs: replacing the curb with a ramp helps those in wheelchairs, but blind people walk out into the traffic."[23]

Yet it is important not to overlook the positive contributions linguistic reforms are bringing into the church. Traditional concepts of God are being enlarged and enriched by new feminine metaphors used to address and speak about God. The "feminization of the church" is bringing dimensions into the heart of the church's life and personality that for centuries have been suffocated by patriarchal attitudes. Members of congregations that have adopted gender-free speech find that it is not as awkward as they had feared and critics had predicted. In fact, they often discover that, with time, a masculine pronoun used

21. Ramshaw, *Worship*, 212.

22. Ruth C. Duck, *Gender and the Name of God: The Trinitarian Baptismal Formula* (New York: Pilgrim Press, 1991), 184. She proposes asking three questions to a baptismal candidate: "Do you believe in God, the Source, the fountain of life? Do you believe in Christ, the offspring of God embodied in Jesus of Nazareth and in the church? Do you believe in the liberating Spirit of God, the wellspring of new life?" (185).

23. Ramshaw, *Worship*, 92–93.

for God comes to sound as awkward as, say, "Negro" used for an African American.

Moreover, as always happens when any part of a group becomes fully incorporated into the whole group, it is the whole group that benefits from the change, not merely the part: The resulting new community is richer and more productive than before. So it is essential that the church continue to make progress. The inclusion of all women and men fully into the sacred speech of the church is fundamental to its nature to be the body of Jesus Christ in and for the world.

Inclusive Lectionaries

Because positions of leadership in the Christian church have been largely reserved for men throughout most of its history, much of what describes the life and practice of the church has been male-oriented. We have been discussing how this situation has affected the language of the church's liturgy. This same situation also has affected the church's lectionaries: because preachers historically have been almost exclusively males, preaching texts have tended to be selected and preached from a decidedly masculine perspective. As a result, lectionaries (lists of texts for preaching through the Bible systematically) generally have overlooked the number and variety of biblical texts that take a feminine perspective.

The more recent lectionaries have addressed and corrected their androcentric bias to some degree. But even the new *Common Lectionary*,[24] a three-year cycle lectionary being used extensively throughout the church, is still not free from a masculine bias (for example, it uses the Genesis 2:18-24 account of the creation of man and woman [Year B, Proper 22], in which God creates Eve from Adam's rib, instead of the 1:26-31 account, in which "male and female God created them"), and it does not even come close to including in its appointed readings the number of texts that tell stories of women of faith and offer feminine images of God. It should be noted, though, that this lectionary is under constant study by the Consultation on Common Texts, and it is likely that the edition scheduled for publication in the fall of 1992 will include additional texts that feature women and feminine viewpoints.

Still, in the interest of including women fully into the church's life, preachers will want to supplement lectionary readings with texts that

---

24. *Common Lectionary* (New York: Church Hymnal Corporation, 1983).

expand the opportunities to preach from a feminine perspective. Ruth Duck has collected twenty-one such texts that are either missing from the *Common Lectionary* or have been appointed for feast days seldom observed by Protestants (and by many Catholics):

1 Sam. 1:3-20: Hannah prays for a son.
1 Sam. 2.1-10: Hannah's prayer for her new son, Samuel.
Isa. 42:14-17: God's intervention in history is like a woman in labor.
Num. 11:10-25: Moses implies that God conceived and gave birth to Israel.
Judg. 11:29-40: Jephthah's daughter consents to be sacrificed.
Gen. 1:26-31: God creates male and female in God's own image.
Luke 19:41-44: Jesus would gather Jerusalem like a mother hen her chicks.
2 Chron. 34:22-33: The prophecy of Huldah to the king of Judah.
Judg. 4:4-9: Deborah, the judge, leads Barak against Sisera.
Mark 14:3-9 (or Matt. 26:6-13): A woman anoints Jesus at Simon's house.
Mark 15:1-47: Women witness Jesus' death.
Acts 9:36-43: The risen Christ raises Tabitha from the dead.
Acts 16:11-15: Lydia, a seller of purple, is converted and baptized.
Matt. 13:33 or Luke 13:20-21: Jesus tells the parable of the Leaven.
John 7:53—8:11: Jesus saves and forgives a woman caught in adultery.
Exod. 15:19-21: Miriam sings as the Israelites pass through the Red Sea.
Acts 18:1-4,18-28: Priscilla and Aquila join up with Paul at Corinth.
Rom. 13:8-10 (omit 1-7): Paul lists a code for Christian living.
Ps. 131: Trusting God is like being "a child at its mother's breast."
Ps. 61:1-5: God is like a rock, a tower, and a shelter.
Esther 4:8-17: Esther goes in before the king to plead for her people.[25]

In addition to incorporating these and other such passages into lectionary readings, preachers will also want to take advantage of the growing number of liturgical resources, preaching helps, and biblical commentaries women of the church are authoring. As Ruth Duck observes, in order to do justice to women in worship, not only is the selection of texts important but feminist interpretations of texts are as well.[26]

---

25. Ruth C. Duck and Maren C. Tirabassi, *Touch Holiness: Resources for Worship* (New York: Pilgrim Press, 1990), 131–34. Suggestions for how these texts may be inserted into the *Common Lectionary* are detailed in the book.

26. Duck and Tirabassi, *Holiness,* 129. For example, see Letty Russell, ed., *Feminine Interpretation of the Bible* (Philadelphia: Westminster Press, 1985); Miriam Therese Winter, *WomanWord: A Feminist Lectionary and Psalter on Women of the New Testament* (New York: Crossroad/Continuum, 1990); idem, *WomanWitness: A Feminist Lectionary and Psalter, Women of the Hebrew Scriptures* (New York: Crossroad/Continuum, 1991); and Carol A. Newsom and Sharon H. Ringe, eds., *The Women's Bible Commentary* (Louisville: Westminster/John Knox, 1992).

Seeking Nondiscriminatory Terminology

We have already underscored the importance of screening out of liturgical speech words that label or stereotype persons. Similarly, it is especially important for the church to use terms that communicate positive and inclusive attitudes toward persons belonging to minority groups. How can the church speak of persons who are handicapped or who are of different races or nationalities or sexual orientations in ways that are affirming and respectful? True, there is much debate in both religious and secular circles about how legitimate this concern is. Some persons (usually belonging to dominant groups) regard the whole matter as irrelevant—an exercise in tiresome hairsplitting.[27] They may charge persons who defend using nondiscriminatory references for minority groups with being politically correct, that is, using the "proper" terminology for political or self-serving reasons. For example, publishers of textbooks are sometimes accused of using inclusive terms as a way to increase sales, and some universities have been criticized for penalizing students for not using "PC language"— that is, language that faculty and administrative officials have determined to be the politically correct way to refer to persons in minority groups.[28]

But controversies over the use of nondiscriminatory language should not obscure the fact that the terms we use for each other influence how we regard and treat each other. If, in a courtroom, a person were to address the judge as "Fred" or "Mrs. Smith," the person would be found in contempt of court for using language inappropriate to a court of law. Why? Not because some arbitrary code of political correctness had been violated, but because the very sanctity and authority of the whole judicial system depends upon a language of formal respect. When Jesus warned his audience against using honorary titles for

27. For example, humorist Lewis Grizzard (*The Commercial Appeal,* 28 January 1991, sec. A, p. 9) complains about "Speech Police" who "are on constant guard against remarks—humorous or otherwise—they consider to fall into those odious categories such as sexism, racism, xenophobia . . . and homophobia," which Grizzard himself regards as much ado about nothing.

28. "Politically correct" language has captured the interest of the political right wing and the news media—feature articles have appeared in *Newsweek, Atlantic, New Republic, New York,* and the *New York Times* (see Leon Howell, "Who's Politically Correct?" *Christianity in Crisis* 51 [10 June 1991]: 187). Unfortunately, "PC" has become another derogatory buzzword, like "welfare" and "quotas," communicating innuendo more than fact.

persons of high social status—"rabbi," "father," "teacher" (Matt. 23:8-10)—was he engaging in so much linguistic nit-picking? Or did he do so because such titles—"doctor," "reverend," "professor"—carry the power to create artificial distinctions of worth among persons who are, in fact, "all brothers and sisters" under "one Father"?

So whether it is true that inclusive terminology is sometimes used for personal or political reasons or not, the church's concern is to use it for the reason that every form of discrimination, including linguistic forms, breeds human pain and creates human oppression, which the church cannot tolerate and must refute. It is not a matter of political correctness; it is a matter of Christian concern for social justice. As one communion has officially stated: "The church is committed to using language in such a way that all members of the community of faith may recognize themselves to be included, addressed, and equally cherished before God. Seeking to bear witness to the whole world, the church struggles to use language which is faithful to biblical truth and which neither purposely nor inadvertently excludes people because of gender, color, or other circumstance in life."[29] So the church, among all institutions in our culture, will lead the way in the search for the most inclusive and beneficent language possible, including the terms used with reference to members of minority groups.

It needs to be said that it is not always necessary to use terms of designation, and that they should be avoided whenever using them may denote stereotyping or bias. For example, to say "the intelligent black student" or "the energetic older person" is to suggest that these are exceptions to the norm. In many cases the ethnic, sexual, religious, or other characteristics of persons are irrelevant to what is being said: for example, "the African American social worker," "the driver of the car, a middle-aged white woman," and "she was mugged by two youths, one Latino and the other Korean." So, distinct references of identification should be avoided when they are not germane to the subject or may be taken as derogatory or stereotypical.[30]

Still, in the church's liturgical speech it is often necessary to refer to distinct groups of persons. Congregations that are sensitive to issues

29. "Directory for Worship," *Book of Order 1989–90* (Louisville: Office of the General Assembly, Presbyterian Church [U.S.A.], 1990): W-1.2006.

30. See *Guidelines for Eliminating Racism, Ageism, Handicappism, and Sexism from United Methodist Resource Materials* (Nashville: United Methodist Publishing House, 1984), 5–7.

of social justice, for example, will need to compare the incomes of women and men in the work force, or to pray for the struggle of Latino migrant workers in cane fields, or to take the side of disabled persons in their efforts to be productive members of society. Congregations that are globally aware will want to weave concerns for Two-Thirds World peoples into their intercessory prayers.

The terms the church uses may well be quite different from terms used in conventional speech—and should be. The church's speech should represent the leading edge of radically inclusive terminology. It is true that the terms themselves often change. Many years ago *colored* was the acceptable term of reference for African Americans, used by African Americans themselves (as in National Association for the Advancement of Colored People), but that term was replaced by *Negro* and then *black,* which is now giving way to *African American.* The church will need to continue making whatever linguistic changes are necessary in order to speak in the most inclusive language possible.

Determining which terms of designation, among the many possibilities, are the most appropriate—that is, which are least discriminatory and most inclusive—is not always a simple matter. The problem is complicated whenever members of minority groups themselves do not agree on the term of preference. Still, as the whole church participates in ongoing discussions about linguistic choices, it can listen to representatives of minority groups, take them seriously, and respond by adapting to the most suitable terminology. These terms might include *African American, lesbians and gay men,* and *Latino.* Instead of using the terms *First World* and *Third World* as global referents, ecumenists are encouraging the use of *One-Third World* and *Two-Thirds World*—terms based on population and land mass instead of levels of economic and industrial development.

If these or any other terms should change with time, then the church's language must change as well. What is important is for the church to honor the terms of designation that underrepresented groups themselves specify as the most nondiscriminatory, and to incorporate these into its liturgical speech.

In conventional speech the United States is frequently referred to as *America.*[31] Yet the United States is, in fact, *of* America, actually of

31. For example, here is one definition of "America": "1. North America. 2. South America. 3. North America, South America, and Central America considered together.

North America, which shares the continent with Central and South Americas. People of the United States who have appropriated the term to apply to themselves exclusively may not have done so because of an inflated sense of self-importance vis-à-vis the other two Americas but because there is no adjectival form for United States (no *United Statesian*), and *American* serves that function. Still, using *America* and *American* as terms for the United States is co-optive and presumptuous and is often perceived by persons in other countries —in the Americas and elsewhere—as another example of United States arrogance, with some justification. Inclusive liturgical speech will honor the nationalities of each country of the Americas by using its particular name, and liturgical speech that is sensitive to international unity will not apply the collective name *America* to any one country *of* the Americas.

Racial and Ethnic Language

At present, the term most often used for designating persons of African descent appears to be *black,* although *African American* is growing in popularity.[32] However, the latter is sometimes criticized by persons on the political and religious right as being the in or politically correct term used primarily by the liberal elite. For example, Craig Bowman, an English teacher at O'Connell Junior High School in Lakewood, Colorado, writes: "For the umpteenth time, I don't want to be called an African-American; I won't use a term that has been imposed by a black 'leadership' that's behaving more and more like the massa every year."[33]

Other terms of designation have not yet reached a consensus. Although *Indian* has been the term generally preferred by American Indians, there is a growing preference for *Native Americans,* especially as the legends and myths of the exploration and conquest of North

4. the United States," the fourth meaning of which is used in the name of the dictionary itself! (*Webster's New World Dictionary of the American Language* [New York: World Publishing Company, 1959].

32. A *Time* magazine poll reports that in February 1989, 61 percent of respondents preferred "black" as the name for their race, and 26 percent preferred "African-American," while, in April 1991, 48 percent preferred "black" and 39 percent preferred "African-American" ("Vox Pop," *Time* 137 [20 May 1991]: 15).

33. Craig Bowman, " 'American,' Thank You; Don't Hyphenate My Heritage," *The Commercial Appeal,* 7 March 1991, sec. A, p. 11. Bowman also does not like the "minority" label, although, he concedes, "it's the best we have."

America become reexamined during the 1992 quincentennial of Columbus's arrival in the Americas.[34] Similarly, *Hispanic,* the term of self-designation generally used by persons of Latin American descent, is giving way to *Latino. Hispanic* literally means "Spanish"—would United States citizens want to be called "English"? Alfonso Roman, chairperson of the Racial Justice Working Group of the National Council of Churches, says, "Latinos come in all colors and shapes, but we do share a Latin American ancestry. As such, the term 'Hispanic' is an inappropriate term for us, used by the dominant society to lump us into their own definition."[35] The term *people of color* is finding increasing usage in church publications and liturgical speech as a more comprehensive term that includes, for example, Asian Americans, Latinos, Native Americans, Spanish, and African Americans.

Inclusive liturgical language will be careful to avoid using black and white as metaphors for bad and good, sin and righteousness. Traditionally, the metaphors have been widely used: devil's food cake is black, angel food cake is white; the black sheep of the family is the rebellious member who has "gone wrong"; black magic is magic used for evil purposes; and if persons are blackballed or blacklisted, they are barred from a group as undesirable. These metaphors can be avoided in liturgical speech. Even darkness and light, prominent biblical metaphors, especially in John's Gospel, can be avoided in sermons by using the realities the metaphors stand for, for example, sin and goodness or evil and godliness.

Some hymn texts in which darkness and black denote evil and sin have been altered in recently published hymnals. For example, in the new Presbyterian hymnal, in the hymn "God Bless Your Church" the line "May we in darkness shine/to light a pathway through life's maze" was changed by substituting "chaos" for "darkness." In the new Methodist hymnal, in the hymn "Have Thine Own Way, Lord" the line "Whiter than snow, Lord,/wash me just now" now reads "Wash me just now, Lord,/wash me just now." One of the advantages of singing

34. In the new United Methodist hymnal, in "O Beautiful for Spacious Skies," the stanza containing the lines, "O beautiful for pilgrim feet,/Whose stern, impassioned stress/A thoroughfare for freedom beat/Across the wilderness," has been eliminated, in deference to Native Americans who were victimized by that "thoroughfare for freedom."

35. Alfonso Roman, "Conflicts of Religion and Real Estate," *Sojourners* 19 (October 1991): 16.

contemporary hymns in worship is that most modern hymnwriters are sensitive to language that is racially demeaning and avoid it in texts they write.

A number of hymnbooks of African American hymns and spirituals have appeared in recent times. Three of the most enthusiastically received are *Songs of Zion*,[36] a collection of multidenominational black hymnody; *AMEC Bicentennial Hymnal*,[37] an extensive collection of music over a wide range of African American traditions, including songs from the AME Church in Africa (and the only black hymnal that shows much concern for nonsexist language); and *Lead Me, Guide Me: The African American Catholic Hymnal*,[38] an eclectic collection of hymns and service music for African American Catholics. In addition, some of the new hymnals for predominantly white churches have significantly increased the number of African American songs, especially spirituals: the United Methodist hymnal contains thirty, the Presbyterian hymnal, twenty, *The Worshiping Church*, fourteen, and the *Psalter Hymnal*, twelve. For a discussion of ethnic hymnody and worship materials, see chapter 5, Incorporating All Cultures.

Persons with Disabilities

Since, in the sight of God, every person is flawed in a variety of ways, one would think that the one place where persons who are physically disabled would feel included would be the church's worship. Yet the language used in worship may possibly cause persons with disabilities to feel isolated or excluded. Especially, persons who do not see, speak, or hear well may experience a lack of involvement in the liturgy or feel that their contribution is secondary. But in various ways, the church can help include them linguistically in worship: by using sign language interpreters or providing hearing aid devices (or adequate amplification) for persons with hearing impairments, by making worship resources available in braille or large print for persons with sight

36. *Songs of Zion* (Nashville: Abingdon Press, 1981).

37. *AMEC Bicentennial Hymnal* (Nashville: African Methodist Episcopal Church, 1984).

38. *Lead Me, Guide Me: The African American Catholic Hymnal* (Chicago: G.I.A. Publications, 1987). For a review of African American hymnals, see Melva Wilson Costen, "Published Hymnals in the Afro-American Tradition," *The Hymn* 40 (January 1989): 7–13.

impairments, and by including the concerns of persons with impairments in sermons and corporate prayers.[39]

The use of gestures and physical movement in worship may increase participation of persons who have speech, sight, or hearing limitations. During prayers, for example, worshipers may be invited to lift up their head, arms, and hands—prayer postures that originate in Jewish worship. Any version of the *orans* position, with arms outstretched, palms up, and head raised, is more expressive of a person's standing before God than the bowed head and clasped hands, which is withdrawn, closed, and inward looking.[40] But the greatest value of movement-prayer is that it broadens the verbal utterance to include physical activity and so invites participation of persons with speech limitations.

Further, leaders of worship can avoid the use of metaphors and images that depict physical disabilities in depreciative ways. They can say, for example, "we shut our eyes to your truth," instead of "we are blind to your truth," "we refuse to listen for your word" instead of "we are deaf to your word," and "we are hindered by old habits" instead of "we are crippled by old habits." This is not always easy to do. Biblical passages frequently use such metaphors: blindness is a recurring metaphor for spiritual hardness of heart (for example, Isa. 42:7; 56:10; 59:10; Matt. 23:16,17; John 9; where the man clearly is blind theologically and physically).

Some of the church's hymns, especially older ones, use imagery that reflects negatively on persons with physical impairments. For example:

> Just as I am, poor, wretched, blind;
> Sight, riches, healing of the mind,
> Yea, all I need, in Thee I find,
> O Lamb of God, I come, I come.

Here, poverty and wretchedness are associated with blindness. In "Amazing Grace" blindness is a metaphor for unbelief: "I once was lost but now am found, was blind but now I see." One stanza of the hymn "O for a Thousand Tongues to Sing" includes a string of disability terminology:

> Hear him ye deaf; his praise, ye dumb,

---

39. See Thomas B. Hoeksema, "One in the Spirit: Involving Persons with Disabilities in Worship," *Reformed Worship* 18 (December 1990): 36–39.

40. See J. G. Davies, *Liturgical Dance: An Historical, Theological and Practical Handbook* (London: SCM Press Ltd., 1984), 164.

Your loosened tongues employ;
Ye blind, behold your Savior come,
And leap, ye lame, for joy.

Yet, where possible, preachers and leaders of worship can re-form their metaphors to avoid depreciative terminology for persons who are physically impaired. Each of the stanzas of the hymns referred to above has been eliminated in the new Presbyterian hymnal because of the negative metaphors.[41] In the hymn "O God, in a Mysterious Way" the phrase "Blind unbelief is sure to err" has been changed to "Our unbelief is sure to err."[42]

We have already seen that terminology used with reference to minority groups is of critical importance, even though determining the proper terms is sometimes difficult. The difficulty with terms commonly used with reference to persons who are disabled—for example, "handicapped," "impaired," "disabled"—is that they carry negative implications. In the field of sports some authorities have tried to remove the negative implications by using terms that sound positive— for example, New York State Park's Games for the Physically Challenged (instead of Disabled) and the Special Olympics (instead of Handicapped Olympics).[43]

However, most organizations that represent disabled persons have rejected awkward and euphemistic attempts to get around negative terminology. In an extensive survey conducted by *The Disability Rag*, a periodical published by a disability advocacy group, terms such as *handi-capable, handicapper,* and *physically challenged* were soundly repudiated by a large majority of readers for being artificial and trivial, and *crippled* for being insensitive and blunt.[44] Other terms rejected were *afflicted, confined, victim,* and *wheelchair-bound* ("without a wheelchair, a person *would* be 'bound' ").[45] The terms of choice in the poll, by far, were *disabled* and *handicapped.*[46]

41. *Presbyterian Hymnal,* 370, 466. ("Amazing Grace," however, was not altered— perhaps because it cannot be.) In the United Methodist hymnal, a footnote to "O for a Thousand Tongues to Sing" indicates that the stanza "may be omitted" (*United Methodist Hymnal,* 57).

42. *Presbyterian Hymnal,* 270. For further discussion on linguistic concerns of the editors of the hymnal, see Sharon K. Youngs, "Textual Concerns," *Reformed Liturgy and Music,* 24 (Winter 1990): 66–68.

43. "N.Y. Program Draws Interest," *USA Today,* 9 May 1991, 2C.

44. "Crips Can Call Themselves Anything They Want To: A Reader Survey," *The Disability Rag* 11 (September/October 1990): 30–33. However, these terms may be used by disabled persons among themselves, as in "Hey, Crip" (33).

45. On a bookmark provided by *The Disability Rag.*

46. The term *physically different person* is sometimes used in the periodical (28). *The Disability Rag* may be subscribed to at Box 145, Louisville, KY 40201.

The use of *differently abled* occasionally appears in church publications and is the term preferred by the World Council of Churches. Yet it finds no support in the poll mentioned above, and, although it does avoid the negative connotations of other terms, it is cumbersome and difficult to use (for example, what term can be used for persons who are *not* differently abled, as in: "All are welcome here—male and female, black and white, rich and poor, differently abled and . . ."?).

The self-advocacy organization People First International recommends that *person* always be used with terms of designation in order to help humanize and soften the reference to disability, and that *person* be placed first. So "persons who have hearing impairments" is preferable to "the deaf" or "the hearing impaired" or "deaf persons," and "persons who are handicapped" is better than "the handicapped" or "handicapped people."[47] Although the suggestion has merit, at times it can make for awkward and forced language, especially when the terms are used in long sentences or when they have to be used repetitively.

Some worshipbooks, in consideration of worshipers who are not physically able to stand up at designated places in the service, suggest that the liturgy read, "All who are able may stand."[48] But surely this is a questionable practice. For one thing, it focuses (unwanted?) attention on the persons who remain seated, and, for another, it singles out one type of disability from many others (should we also invite "all who are able" to sing the hymn or say the creed or listen to the reading of scripture?).

Worship leaders will continue to search for the most inclusive and nondiscriminatory terminology possible with reference to persons who are disabled, language that both affirms their presence and celebrates their contributions and unique gifts.

Language about Age

Conversational language almost inevitably necessitates references to persons of distinct age levels: infants, children, teenagers, young adults, mature adults, and so on. The term of choice for persons who have

47. Cited in Hoeksema, "One in the Spirit," 38.
48. For example, *The Book of Worship: United Church of Christ.*

advanced beyond middle age is *older adults* or *older persons,* not *senior citizens* or *golden agers.* Some church publications are using the term *Third Age* (that is, the last general stage of a normal life span: young, middle, old) as in, "Third Age resources" or "opportunities for Third Age persons to serve," but this term at least approximates being a euphemism. Persons who have retired from their professional occupations prefer to be referred to as *retired persons* or *persons who have retired,* not as *retirees* or *the retired* or *nonemployed.*

Liturgical speech must guard against stereotyping persons within certain age categories and will recognize that there are exceptions to all generalities: all older adults are not wise, disciplined, and in bad health, all teenagers are not naïve, undisciplined, and in good health; not all children are precocious; not all retired persons are inactive or have free time (in fact, they may not even be older adults—many now retire at middle age).

The United Methodist Church has compiled guidelines with reference to age distinctions for writers of its resource materials that could apply to spoken language as well.[49] From that material I have drawn up these general guidelines:

1. Avoid language that stereotypes persons or is based upon unsupported generalizations about any age group.
2. Avoid patronizing language about any age group.
3. Avoid language that implies that any church class, congregation, or agency is inferior, superior, inefficient, or more efficient simply because it has a predominance of younger or older members.
4. Do not talk "down" to young people—avoid speaking of adolescent persons as children.
5. Characterize persons of all age levels realistically, not idealistically.

Most hymnals either have a section containing hymns for children and young people or designate such hymns in the topical index. Thomas Shepard says that "there is no music that is pastorally, liturgically, and musically sound for adult communities that cannot also be used with children."[50] Still, the images, language, and subject matter of some hymns obviously are more relevant to children's experience than others, and the tunes of some are more singable.

---

49. *Guidelines,* 8–11.
50. Thomas B. Shepard, "What Does It Mean to Be a Child?" in Virgil C. Funk, ed., *Children, Liturgy, and Music* (Washington, D.C.: Pastoral Press, 1990), 76.

Few hymnals designate hymns that apply expressly to older adults.[51] The American Association of Retired Persons has published *Ten New Hymns on Aging and the Later Years*, which is still available to churches,[52] but the hymns have received only limited use. Although most general hymns might be considered age-neutral, oriented toward no specific age group, certain hymns are more amenable to the theme of aging, especially to the stages of life and the passing of time. Certain psalms fit this category: 23, 71, 90, 92, 103, and 148. William S. Smith has suggested other hymns:

"O God, Our Help in Ages Past"
"Great God, We Sing that Mighty Hand"
"Rejoice, Ye Pure in Heart"
"Guide Me, O Thou Great Jehovah"
"If Thou But Suffer God to Guide Thee"
"Jesus, Lead the Way"
"God of Our Life, Through All the Circling Years"[53]

There is no reason why a congregation composed of different age groups cannot share in each others' hymns and other liturgical expressions. The important thing is for the whole congregation to participate communally, not each group doing only that which is appropriate to itself. In general, the church's speech will aim at building respect, appreciation, and affection among and between the generations. It will "reflect the way the Bible treats persons—as distinct individuals with strengths, weaknesses, and divine callings, which are not determined by age."[54]

Nonviolent Language

The United States is unquestionably among the most violent nations in the world. More teenage males die from gunfire than from all natural causes combined. In 1990 twelve major cities set new records for the number of homicides—there are about 30,000 homicides in the United

---

51. The *Psalter Hymnal* has the entry "Aging: see 'Brevity & Frailty of Life.' "
52. See Selected Resources, under "Hymnbooks."
53. William S. Smith, "Hymns Related to Aging," *The Hymn* 40 (October 1989): 29.
54. *Guidelines,* 11.

States each year.[55] The sale of war toys abounds at Christmas. One of the most powerful and feared lobbies in the nation is the National Rifle Association, whose raison d'être is the promotion of guns. Motion picture and television entertainment, drenched in gratuitous blood and gore, communicates the message that brute force resolves human conflicts. About one half of the United States budget is military related. Hodding Carter III, a syndicated columnist, says, "What exists in fact rather than theory for the U.S. in the latter half of the 20th century is a permanent state of war, marked by regular outbursts of sustained fighting and occasional uneasy ceasefires."[56]

It is not surprising that conventional speech reflects this violence. Some of our favorite metaphors, especially when speaking about effort or power or challenge, are military. If somebody wants to ask us a question, we might tell them to "shoot" or "fire away." When corrected for something we did or said, we might say that we got "blown away" or "shot down." Our ideas get "bombed," our plans get "torpedoed," and our teams get "blitzed." A reporter "targets" a story toward an audience—and if the editor does not like the story, she might "kill it." Overheard in a theatre lobby: "I'd kill for a body like that!"

In light of the words and work of the Prince of Peace, violent language ought to seem as out of place in a service of Christian worship as vulgar or scatological language. Yet, strangely, it is often as at home in our churches as anywhere else. In prayer and sermon God might be enlisted variously to help "attack prejudice," "fight greed," or "take up arms against evil" (should we "do battle against war" and "fight every form of violence"?). One author suggests that a sermon should be like a bullet "designed to hit the hearer in one vital spot," instead of bird shot that "spray[s] him with scattered theological ideas . . . in a dozen places."[57] Churches may even sing in the language of violence: in one hymnal, in the section "Life in Christ: Loyalty and Courage," these militaristic hymns appear, almost back-to-back:

55. According to The Day America Told the Truth, by James Patterson and Peter Kim, the homicide rate among young American males is twenty times that of Western Europe and forty times the Japanese rate. Guns were used in three-fourths of the killings in America versus one-fourth of those in other industrialized nations (cited in The Commercial Appeal, 7 July 1991, sec. E, p. 4). In 1990 more people were killed by guns in Texas (3,443) than from automobile accidents (3,309) (The Commercial Appeal, 9 November 1991, sec. A, p. 1).

56. Cited in The Washington Spectator 17 (1 April 1991): 3.

57. Donald Miller, Way to Biblical Understanding (Nashville: Abingdon Press, 1957), 53.

"God Is My Strong Salvation; What Foe Have I to Fear?"
"Stand Up, Stand Up for Jesus, Ye Soldiers of the Cross"
"Onward, Christian Soldiers, Marching as to War"
"March On, O Soul, with Strength!"
"Am I a Soldier of the Cross, a Follower of the Lamb?"
"The Son of God Goes Forth to War, a Kingly Crown to Gain"
"Who Is on the Lord's Side? Who Will Serve the King?"[58]

It may be a sign of our time that, when the hymnal revision committee of the United Methodist Church considered eliminating "Onward Christian Soldiers" from its new hymnal because of its militarism, some members of the committee received death threats.[59]

Does this really matter? Does using metaphors of violence in positive ways in worship adversely affect worshipers? Does it foster attitudes of violence? At the very least the use of violent language in the church certainly legitimizes similar language in movies, television, popular music, and literature. It condones linguistically what the church condemns theologically. A language of violence contributes to a climate of violence. The casual use of military-related metaphors helps normalize the realities behind the metaphors, and when used in the liturgical language of the church, grants those realities a certain status, an acceptability. Is it even conceivable that we would use images and metaphors of sexual pathology—incest, masochism, nymphomania, prostitution—in our sermons, prayers, and hymns? Why not?

It is true that military metaphors and images appear frequently in biblical texts: Acts 5:39, Romans 13:12, 2 Timothy 4:7, Hebrews 10:32, and especially Ephesians 6. Each issue of *Full Armor*, a magazine for U.S. military personnel published by The Brotherhood Commission of the Southern Baptist Convention, carries a column that relates Bible verses to the military. In one issue, "the sword of the Spirit" in Ephesians 6:17 is linked metaphorically to the "smart weapons" used in the war against Iraq: "To have the sword of the Spirit is to have the Word of God. To be armed with this weapon is to take into battle the ultimate of smart weapons."[60] It would be difficult to argue that that military metaphor does not condone, if not glorify, war.

58. *The Hymnbook* (Richmond: Presbyterian Church in the United States, The United Presbyterian Church in the U.S.A., Reformed Church in America, 1960). The military metaphor is used in seven out of the ten hymns in this section.

59. Grindal, "Inclusive Language," 191.

60. John Beifuss, "Baptist Magazine Targeted at Troops," *The Commercial Appeal,* 3 June 1991, sec. B, p. 1.

Not even the biblical use of military images should keep the Christian church from facing the possibility that, especially in today's world, the speech of violence may have a negative impact on society by encouraging, or at least sanctioning, violent attitudes and behavior. Peace activist Gerard A. Vanderhaar advocates speaking in "a new dialect"—a language that replaces conventional violence-oriented terms with terms more appropriate to a Christian vocabulary: "A nonviolent person eventually has to learn what is almost another language. It's not entirely new, but the kind of variation on common usage that's called a dialect. It tries to avoid words that convey images of violence, and instead uses phrases that are either neutral or positively supportive. We want to mitigate the aura of violence, not reinforce it."[61] In our speech, he says, we can substitute metaphors: "Instead of 'We've got to get it in our sights' we could say, 'Let's keep our eyes on the prize.' An expression 'Kill two birds with one stone' can become 'Feed two birds with one crust.' "[62]

As much as possible, liturgical speech ought to mirror theological belief. Although it is impossible to make that reflection perfectly—we do, after all, "see through a glass darkly"—we can work toward that goal, monitoring our speech, discussing (even debating!) the issues and problems involved. We can make progress. For example, of the seven hymns cited above that use militaristic metaphors in an earlier Presbyterian hymnal, six have been omitted from the new Presbyterian hymnal, and four do not appear in the new United Methodist hymnal.[63] The Presbyterian hymnal has reduced to a footnote the two most graphically violent stanzas in "For All the Saints," a hymn that calls to mind the bloody warfare of the Crusades. Further, Kathleen Hughes has shown how modern Catholic liturgy has been influenced by a renewed concern for a language of peace. Comparing prayers from

61. Gerard A. Vanderhaar, *Active Nonviolence: A Way of Personal Peace* (Mystic, Conn.: Twenty-Third Publications, 1990), 26.

62. Vanderhaar, *Nonviolence,* 27. A notable example: When Boris Becker, the German tennis star, won his first Wimbledon championship at age seventeen, journalists wanted to dub him "Boom Boom" because of his powerful serve and ground strokes. But Becker said, "No, please. I want nothing about war or shooting connected with my name." The nickname was dropped (television sportscaster Bud Collins, "Wimbledon Tennis: Men's Finals," 7 July 1991, NBC).

63. The Presbyterian hymnal also provides an alternative version of "A Mighty Fortress Is Our God," by Omer Westendorf. See Youngs, "Textual Concerns," 266–68.

the English-Latin Roman Missal of Pius V [A, below] and the post-consiliar Missal of Paul VI [B, below], she finds a shift in prayer language toward "a Church no longer self-righteous and vindictive, a Church that recognizes that violence and cruelty are not of God, a Church that fears weapons of hate."

[A] O God, you destroy wars and by your power you overthrow the aggressors of those who hope in you. Help your servants who appeal to you, so that we may overcome our belligerent enemies and never cease to praise and thank you. Through Jesus Christ. . . .

[B] God of power and mercy, you destroy wars and put down earthly pride. Banish violence from our midst and wipe away our tears that we may all deserve to be called your sons and daughters. We ask this. . . .

[A] Almighty and eternal God, your hand controls the power and government of every nation. Help your Christians and by the might of your right hand destroy the nonbelieving peoples who rely on their own cruel strength. Through Jesus Christ. . . .

[B] God our Father, you reveal that those who work for peace will be called your sons [and daughters]. Help us to work without ceasing for that justice which brings true and lasting peace. We ask this. . . .[64]

Undeniably, the "principalities and powers, the cosmic powers of this age" that the writer of Ephesians warns us about (6:12) are formidable enough to call for using the most powerful language available in withstanding their evil. So we wrestle (as the passage begins), struggle, contend, strive, and vie with them; we resist, confront, withstand, defy, counteract, and oppose them. But the language of liturgy will reflect what in the last analysis we know to be true: the Christian way is the way of nonviolent resistance. So we will speak in images and metaphors of nonviolence, in the hope that a language of nonviolence will contribute to a climate of nonviolence.

Sexuality

The question arises about whether matters of human sexuality should be a concern of the church's liturgical language. The "s-word" is rarely mentioned in worship—the church's liturgical speech tends to be as

---

64. H. Kathleen Hughes, "The Voice of the Church at Prayer," in Kathleen Hughes and Mark R. Francis, eds., *Living No Longer for Ourselves: Liturgy and Justice in the Nineties* (Collegeville, Minn.: The Liturgical Press, 1991), 105.

celibate as the Catholic priesthood. What does the church imply about its contemporary relevance, when sexual language more or less common to most other areas of our culture is practically nonexistent in the church's worship? True, not every topic discussed by Oprah or Geraldo on television during the week needs to show up in the liturgy on Sunday in order for the church to be socially relevant, yet there is something disturbing about the church's reluctance even to mention liturgically what is so much a part of life socially. One reason for the absence of sexual concerns in liturgical language must be that historically the church has been ambiguous about how it regards sex—as sinful, dangerous, a biological necessity, or as altogether personal and therefore private. Another reason may be that current sexual practices and attitudes are so fluid and pluralistic, even among Christians, that the church can say very little about human sexuality that is definitive or unequivocal.[65] Opinions about such matters as sex roles, homosexuality, divorce and remarriage, sex outside marriage, single-parent families, and sexually explicit art vary so widely among Christians and have created such heated controversies that it can be problematic even to frame prayer petitions without offending persons or appearing to be judgmental.

Congregations vary, obviously, and what is allowed to be spoken in worship will depend largely on a particular congregation's sensitivities. Yet even more conservative congregations might allow at least the use of euphemistic language with reference to sex, so that, for example, if thanking God "for the gift of sexual intimacy" might be offensive, then thanking God "for the gift of *human* intimacy" might be acceptable. Other thanksgivings:

- "for marriage; for the mystery and joy of flesh made one."[66]
- for physical and spiritual attraction of person to person, through which relationships are formed and intimacy is shared.

65. As a case in point, see the debate that erupted over the report of the Special Committee on Human Sexuality of the Presbyterian Church (U.S.A.), "Keeping Body and Soul Together: Sexuality, Spirituality, and Social Justice" (1987). For a discussion of the church and sexual issues, see Marvin M. Ellison, "Common Decency: A New Christian Sexual Ethics," *Christianity and Crisis* 50 (12 November 1990): 352–56. Also, see the booklet "Sexual Ethics and the Church: After the Revolution," published by the Christian Century Foundation (407 S. Dearborn Street, Chicago, IL 60605).

66. *The Worshipbook: Services and Hymns* (Philadelphia: Westminster Press, 1970), 114.

- for the handshakes of strangers, the smiles of friends, the hugs of families, and the bodies of lovers.[67]

The fact remains that human sexuality is an area of human existence that can be both troubled and troubling and so needs our prayerful intercessions. Here are some efforts at framing rather careful liturgical intercessions that might be included in a general prayer, depending on the sensitivities of a particular congregation:

- for persons seeking to express their sexual nature in loving and responsible ways.
- for persons who are struggling to discover their sexual identity.
- for those who fear the risk of human intimacy and so miss its beauty and blessing.
- for the church's ministry to persons who strive to grow creatively in relationships of tenderness, affection, and loving intimacy.
- cure those who abuse their God-given gift of sexuality, and heal those who have been abused.
- we remember before you:
  persons who have been sexually harassed, persons who are treated as sex objects, persons who use sex selfishly for personal advantage.

Attending to Congregational Inclusiveness

Once a congregation recognizes the variety of persons and distinct groups that make up its membership, it can represent that variety inclusively in its liturgical speech. Leaders of worship need to be sensitive to the minority groups of the congregation, or else the language of the liturgy will exclusively represent the majority personality or the predominant social class. If a congregation is composed predominantly of white, middle-aged, blue-collar, working-class adults, the possibility exists that the needs, problems, and interests characterizing that group become the ones most often voiced in the language of worship. That is to say, whatever the constituency of the predominant groups might be—suburban affluent or intercity poor, retired persons or young people, single persons or families, working class or leisure class, and so on—it is possible for a congregation's liturgical

67. Adapted from Chris Glaser, *Coming Out to God: Prayers for Lesbians and Gay Men, Their Families and Friends* (Louisville: Westminster/John Knox, 1991), 102.

language to express the interests of predominant segments to the neglect of others.

But if this should happen, a subtle form of exclusion takes place. The linguistic imbalance favoring predominant groups causes the needs, problems, and interests of underrepresented persons to seem less important and so to be at the periphery of the church's life. Overlooked minorities generally take the situation in stride, but not always. For example, a United Methodist Church in downtown Memphis recently organized a new congregation composed of single persons (called the "Singles Church"). The organizers had planned for 50 persons on the first Sunday, but 80 showed up. The next Sunday there were 150 in the congregation, and then 190, and last Sunday, as this is being written, more than 200. Granted, this kind of specialized congregation (like special masses in the Catholic church) is hardly desirable since it splits up congregations into discrete groups, yet members of the new Singles Church argue that they are leaving specialized congregations—that is, congregations made up predominantly of couples and families. Does the liturgical language of those family-oriented churches include the interests, needs, and life-styles of the members who are single?

Similarly, a number of denominations and religious groups in the United States are directing their ministries primarily to avowed gay men and lesbians. The United Metropolitan Community Church, along with denominational groups such as Dignity (Catholic), Integrity (Episcopal), Affirmation (United Methodist), and GLAD (Disciples of Christ), are made up primarily of persons whose sexual orientation has alienated them, in one way or another, from their home churches. Is this because gay men and lesbians have been linguistically excluded or unrepresented in the worship of the mainstream congregations?

So the language of a congregation's liturgy will find ways of representing the wide range of life characteristics of the various types and groups of persons among whom it is being spoken. Liturgies will contain language that reflects the old as well as the young, children as well as adults (teenagers, too, are a separate and special age division), women as well as men, both blue-collar and white-collar workers, single persons as well as families, persons of different races, life-styles, and so on. Sermon content, illustrations and stories, as well as prayer confessions, thanksgivings, petitions and intercessions, can incorporate the pluralistic character of the congregation. For example, when sermon illustrations involve persons, the persons can vary among women and men, married and single, children and adults, lower income and higher income. The illustrations also can include situations that are descriptive of a wide scope of human experience. Prayers of thanksgiving can include blessings uniquely experienced, for example, by the sick as well as the healthy, by persons who are single and others who have families, by persons who work and others who have retired; and particular intercessions can represent the assortment of needs experienced variously throughout the church community. Some of the prayers in *The Worshipbook* aim for this kind of inclusiveness. In the "Litany of Thanksgiving," thanksgivings are given for persons in distinct age groups: "For children; for their energy and curiosity; for their brave play and their startling frankness; for their sudden sympathies; for the young; for their high hopes; for their irreverence toward worn-out values; their search for freedom; their solemn vows; for growing up and growing old; for wisdom deepened by experience; for rest in leisure; and for time made precious by its passing."[68] In a "Litany for Those Who Work," petitions are made for persons whose type of work is named explicitly:

> For those who plow the earth,
> For those who tend machinery;
> For those who work in offices and warehouses,
> For those who labor in stores or factories;
> For those who entertain us,
> For those who broadcast or publish;
> For those who keep house,
> For those who train children;
> For all who employ or govern;
> For all who excite our minds with art, science, or learning.[69]

Vienna Cobb Anderson has written a book of prayers that addresses a remarkably diverse number of needs and situations coming from her own pastoral experience. She "filled the gap" in her denominational prayerbook with prayers that "relate to issues that affect us all: child abuse, violent crime, rape, terrorism, divorce, and AIDS, to name but a few."[70] For example:

68. *Worshipbook*, 114–15.
69. *Worshipbook*, 130–31.
70. Vienna Cobb Anderson, *Prayers of Our Hearts in Word and Action* (New York: Crossroad, 1991), xi.

Prayers for Women Who Have Had a Miscarriage
Prayer for Children Going to School
Prayer for Those Who Hate Their Parents
Prayer for Our Enemies
Prayer for Those Who Despair of Living
Prayer for Those Learning to Be Single
Prayer for Abused Men
Prayer for a Friend Who Erred
Prayer for a Forthcoming Election
Prayer of a Woman Facing the Choice of Abortion
For My Best Friend Who Has Moved Away
A Ritual for Rebuilding Memories after a Fire
Blessing for a Couple Who Are Getting a Divorce[71]

In one worship service, as a part of the Great Prayer of Thanksgiving before communion, the celebrant included this thanksgiving:

Thank you for the world so sweet,
thank you for the food we eat,
thank you for the birds that sing,
thank you God, for everything.

The inclusion of this child's prayer reminded adult worshipers of children's presence in the assembly and of their unique contribution to the church's life; there is no way to know exactly what it meant to the children, except that, surely, it made them conscious of their being included as participants in the eucharistic celebration.

Another congregation regularly includes children's songs in the liturgy: one Sunday, along with the hymn "For the Beauty of the Earth," worshipers sang, "Jesus Loves the Little Children, All the Children of the World." Also, using children and youth choirs in worship demonstrates the church's concern for inclusiveness and incorporates a musical contribution into the liturgy that only they can make (provided, of course, it is not primarily a performance).[72] Still another

---

71. Anderson, *Prayers,* v–x.

72. For a discussion of children's music in congregational worship, see Virgil C. Funk, *Children, Liturgy, and Music* (Washington, D.C.: Pastoral Press, 1990). Practical suggestions for including children in all aspects of the Sunday liturgy can be found in: Roger Gobbel and Phillip Huber, *Creative Designs with Children at Worship* (Louisville: Westminster/John Knox, 1981); Jack Miffleton, *Sunday's Child: A Planning Guide for Liturgies with both Children and Adults* (Washington, D.C.: Pastoral Press, 1989); and Carolyn C. Brown, *Forbid Them Not: Involving Children in Sunday Worship* (Nashville: Abingdon Press, 1991).

church community, in consideration of the number of single persons participating in worship, began using less family-oriented language; for example, by changing family night activities to church-wide activities, speaking of the church more as community than as family, and including unmarried, divorced, and widowed persons in worship activities such as lighting the Advent wreath.

In addition to the examples provided above, here are prayer petitions that aim at expressing congregational inclusivity. Thanksgivings might be given:

- for bright sunny days and cool dark nights; for trees to climb and parks to play in.
- for work to do when we are well, and for nurses to care for us when we are sick.
- for cities with their shops and skyscrapers, restaurants and theaters, and for country places with their fields and farms, village stores and town squares.
- for things to do and friends to do them with; for places to go and friends who want to go with us.
- for the startling curiosity of youth, and for the seasoned wisdom of age.
- for the pleasure of solitude—for being alone without being lonely.
- for having friends and falling in love; for persons all around us whom we share ourselves with and who share themselves with us.
- for persons who talk with us when we are lonely, who help us up when we fall, and who receive us back when we fail.
- for football and basketball and paintings and poems; for rock music and Bach music.

The thanksgivings below were gleaned from a newspaper column that appeared on Thanksgiving Day:

- for long journeys safely concluded, noisy family reunions, and the quiet when everybody has left.
- for amateur theater and high school sports.
- for libraries and bookstores, bicycle shops and hardware stores; for rummage sales and cafes that offer good talk.
- for all who have to work during holidays.
- for old histories, almanacs, maps, Bibles, and McGuffey's Readers.
- for bluegrass and country and blues and swing and jazz.
  For music that's more than the notes. For combos and small-town symphonies and Concertgebouw. For Patsy Cline and Mozart.

- for anybody who ever taught anybody else to read or helped the Salvation Army.

- for neighbors who are still neighbors, knowing when to appear and when to disappear.

- for good ol' boys and girls and auto mechanics who know what they're doing; for cooks and barbers and printers and shoe repairers and others who take pride in their work; for the secretaries and non-coms who run the world.

- for the hope of youth, the wisdom of age; for every child's clear, quick sense of justice and those adults who honor it.

- for those who study the issues and candidates, support their favorites, and are sure to vote.

- for persons who seek no credit, have no slick line to sell, who do their work without compromise or folderol.[73]

Inclusive intercessions might be:

- bless and help people in their work: at the office, in department stores, at home, at school; in warehouses and service stations, in court houses and restaurants; those who must travel.

- we remember those who serve our church: Sunday school teachers, ushers and acolytes, those who clean and care for the building, people who help us sing, those who prepare the bread and wine for your table.

- for those who have been wounded in the struggles of life: by injustice, by their own limitations, or by some uncontrollable circumstance.

- for persons who have too little time for play and leisure, and for those who have too much.

- for persons who have been pushed to the margins of society, and for persons who are trying to live on shrinking incomes and inadequate food or shelter.

- for those who cannot work, and those who cannot work; for persons who are underpaid, and persons who seek to be overpaid.

The church serves as the body of Christ in the world by refusing to honor the subtle systems of caste, class, race, sex, age, ethnic origin, and any other artificial distinction within the human family of God observed by popular culture. In its worship the church will use speech that encompasses a wide range of human distinctions and differences.

73. Paul Greenberg, "A Bevy of Reasons for One to Be Thankful," *The Commercial Appeal,* 22 November 1990, sec. A, p. 9.

It refuses to use terms or expressions that alienate, stereotype, label, or exclude. Discriminatory language does not merely offend persons or hurt their feelings; it wounds, hurts, and abuses persons, it attacks the core of their selfhood. In a society that divides persons into homogenous groups, the church builds heterogeneous communities. The one place in the whole social order where persons should be able to count on being accepted, respected, and loved, no matter who or what they are, is the community of the faithful who represent the body of Christ in the world.

5

Incorporating
All Cultures

The language of the church's liturgies must go beyond representing the diversity within its own membership. Bonhoeffer said that as Christians we throw ourselves into the arms of God "and participate in his sufferings in the world and watch with Christ in Gethsemane. That is faith, that is *metanoia* (repentance), and that is what makes a man and a Christian."[1] Because the church is in and for the world, its liturgical speech will reflect that it is engaged with a far greater range of human concerns than those of a single congregation. Here again, we can speak of the church's worldly language, since each particular congregation does not worship exclusively for and by itself but vicariously with its surrounding culture.

Struggling toward Global Inclusiveness

Yet Christian churches in One-Third World countries have been painfully slow to participate in the ongoing struggles of the rest of the world. Robert Hovda writes:

> Our ruts and our habits and our predetermined ways and the structures of our society have fastened such blinders on our harnesses that, as a whole, Christians and Christian churches in our society have only the haziest notion of any moral imperative flowing from the Sunday meeting in which we celebrate God's word of human liberation and solidarity, and then act it out in the breaking of the bread and the sharing of the cup.

---

1. Cited in Martin Marty, "Bonhoeffer: Seminarians' Theologian," *Christian Century* 77 (20 April 1960): 469. No reference cited.

As obvious as those ethical demands are, they simply do not impinge, they do not get through to us. We are too well protected by the world we live in.[2]

In Romans, Paul says that not merely individual persons or congregations, or nations or continents, but "the whole creation has been groaning in labor pains until now" awaiting its redemption (8:22). Individual congregations, then, will not be indifferent to worldwide conditions but will identify with them: in their celebrations and their trials, in their failures and their successes, being aware of their problems, sacrificing in behalf of their needs, rejoicing in their accomplishments. The familiar saying of John Wesley might apply to all pastors and congregations: "I look upon the world as my parish."

The Christian church has employed various means of engaging in its world mission: social agencies, missionary programs, relief work, and welfare organizations. Our concern here is that the speech of the church's worship also reflect this engagement. In some cases, congregations participate vigorously in community and global ministries, put funding for relief work in their budgets, and inform study groups about critical conditions worldwide, yet do not speak of these global concerns in their worship.

This is a surprising and surely an abnormal situation. Because language matters, the church's participation in global events needs to be spoken in its corporate worship. Ours is a time when new global flash points seem to break out like viruses almost daily: the business of the worshiping community is constantly to speak to these crises in its sermons and to pray in behalf of them in its prayers. The speech of the church joins and reinforces the work the church does in global ministry. Leaders of liturgy, like the prophets of Israel, both speak to the people in behalf of God and to God in behalf of the people.

So the church will voice its concern along with Paul that "the creation itself will be set free from its bondage to decay and will obtain the freedom of the glory of the children of God" (8:21). Through their liturgical prayers, worshipers will look out over the world, and wherever they see evidences of God at work for good, will speak the language of celebration. Wherever they see human acts of evil at work against God, like Jesus weeping over Jerusalem, they will cry out

2. Robert Hovda, "The Mass and Its Social Consequences," *Liturgy 90* 22 (April 1991): 10.

words of lament. Wherever they see the oceans of human deprivation, injustice, and oppression, they will speak the language of intercession, sometimes in reverent tones of hope, sometimes in angry cries of despair. In all of its sacred speech, the church's liturgies will be inclusive of the realities of its larger parish, the world.

After World War II, Coventry Cathedral in England was rebuilt next to the bombed-out hulk of the building it replaced. The new cathedral is magnificent. Inside, worshipers are surrounded by brick walls eighty feet high, an immense tapestry hanging above the altar, and stunning stained glass windows that reach from floor to ceiling. But there is something more. The cathedral's chapel thrusts out from the side of the nave in a large semicircle, high above the ground. Only here there are no tapestries or stained glass. The wall of the entire semicircle is a window of clear glass from floor to ceiling. Looking through it, worshipers get a panoramic view of a large section of the city. Close by is a neighborhood made up of neat, modest homes. But that neighborhood, as it is followed on out toward the horizon, gradually deteriorates, becoming what is obviously a part of the slums of Coventry. In the distance, shaping the horizon, is a chain of giant factories pouring out smoke that darkens the sky. The cathedral's architect wanted us to worship God in the beauty of the cathedral where the world's ugliness is shut from sight, but also to worship God in the chapel, where we must look straight into the afflictions of our sisters and brothers and know that, somehow, the church exists for them.

So when the speech spoken and heard in the church's worship is inclusive speech, it serves to gather up within its own community the needs of all humanity, not only the more acceptable, seemly, or popular segments. Again, Jesus of the Gospels is our model. His care went out to prostitutes, tax collectors, outcast lepers, and reprobate Samaritans as much as to the more respectable needy. Jesus freely touched the untouchables, but how often does the church's language embrace present-day untouchables? Too often the pitiable state of people such as drug users and pushers, rapists, terrorists, and child abusers, are unrepresented in the prayers of God's people at worship. While the church needs to remember before God the innocent victims of crimes and injustice, radical Christian prayer will remember the guilty perpetrators as well. Recently, author John Cheever's personal journal was published posthumously. One entry reads:

> Waiting in the police station to pay a parking ticket, I hear on the radio that a middle-aged man, slight build, five feet seven, brown hair, is wanted for open lewdness. He unzipped his trousers at the corner of Elm Avenue and Chestnut Street and did the same thing twenty minutes later in front of the A. & P. . . . A five-state alarm is out; and where can he be? Reading "Tommy Titmouse" to his children. Hiding in a garage, or a movie theatre. Drinking in a bar. I pray for him, among others, in church.[3]

The nature of public worship being what it is, it is not likely that a public prayer for the man in Cheever's story would be considered appropriate. Still, Cheever's personal intercession exemplifies a Christian concern for the kind of person generally considered to be not even within the scope of human tolerance, let alone the object of prayer. The prayers of the church can include persons who are excluded everywhere else.

Our liturgical intercessions will include our enemies. It is surprising to note how seldom the church's prayers include petitions for the one category of persons Jesus explicitly directed us to pray for: "But I say to you, love your enemies and pray for those who persecute you, so that you may be children of your Father in heaven" (Matt. 5:44,45). In ordinary speech, enemies—persons or groups or nations we perceive to oppose us or to seek our harm or even our destruction—generally receive words of reproach. But sacred speech is not ordinary: so our prayers will include our enemies.

One Sunday, a parish minister included in his pastoral prayer an intercession "for persons and nations whom we fear or who we perceive to be our enemies," and went on to name examples: "such as the nations of Libya, Cuba, and the Soviet Union, and members of the Palestine Liberation Organization." Now this happened during the time President Reagan was publicly referring to Russia as "an evil empire," and when the time came in the prayer for the congregation to respond with, "In your mercy, O God, hear our prayer," there was considerable hesitation and not much sound. On her way out after the service, a lady said to the minister, "Well, that's the first time I've ever been asked to pray for the Communists." The minister replied (in quasi-Rogerian fashion), "Well, how did you feel about it?" She answered, "To tell the truth, I was surprised . . . I guess sort of shocked." She paused, sighed, and then added, "Of course, I know: Jesus did *tell* us to pray for our enemies." Such was her reluctant, yet

---

3. John Cheever, "Journals (Part 2)," *The New Yorker* (13 August 1990): 44.

candid, acknowledgment that the church's prayers should include even our enemies.[4]

Yet we do not include unpopular persons and enemies in our prayers merely out of dutiful obedience to a command of Jesus; we include them because, when we do, we extend an expression of the all-encompassing and unconditional love of God that is beyond what is easy and conventional to become an expression of the radical nature of that love. To pray for enemies is at the same time to solicit their forgiveness; naming enemies before God is to seek their reconciliation.

Bonhoeffer reminds us that "there is no part of the world, be it never so forlorn and never so godless, which is not accepted by God and reconciled with God in Jesus Christ."[5] So the church's speech will be in behalf of the unpopular: persons and groups political parties will not include for fear it would cost them votes, those whose social life-styles brand them as outcasts, persons whom the news media label undesirables, or at least, undeservables, and persons who are too liberal to be tolerated by conservatives or too conservative to be tolerated by liberals. It will represent the needs of social untouchables and of enemies.

Here are some specific examples of liturgical prayer language designed to be globally inclusive. Intercessions might be offered:

- for all who suffer famine and epidemic.

- for refugees longing for their homelands, and migrant workers trying to survive yet one more day.

- for the sick and dying: especially for those who suffer from AIDS and other life-threatening diseases.

- for children everywhere who have been abused or assaulted, who are sick or hungry or poor, or who are the victims of war.

- for children and teenagers who are attacked by Israeli soldiers because they are Palestinian; for people in South Africa who are persecuted because they are black; and for missionaries in Guatemala who are persecuted because they follow Christ's commands.

---

4. Similarly, when Terry Anderson was released after being held hostage for six and a half years in Lebanon, he said this in reference to his captors (*Los Angeles Times,* 7 December 1991, sec. A, p. 20): "I don't hate anybody. I'm a Christian and a Catholic, and I really believe that. And it's required of me that I forgive, no matter how hard that may be. And I'm determined to do that."

5. Cited in Marty, "Bonhoeffer," 469.

- for those who run soup kitchens in the Sudan, halfway houses in Haiti, and storefront missions in Cuba; those who harbor the persecuted in China, and who comfort the dying in Calcutta.
- for all prisoners, especially political prisoners and those who are innocent of any crime, and for those whose sentences are unjust.
- for criminals and all who have committed acts against society; for those who have nobody to pray for them.
- for victims of cruelty and injustice, and for those who commit cruelty and injustice.
- for persons we find difficult to love, and for persons who find it difficult to love us.
- for our enemies: nations whose government we oppose politically or militarily, such as Iran, Iraq, Cuba, and Libya.
- for nations of the world whom our nation resents or looks down on or considers to be inferior or subject to our control.
- for nations whose leaders seem distrustful and hostile toward us, and for nations toward whom our leaders seem distrustful and hostile.

Because Christ died for the whole world, the whole world is included in the life and mission of the church. The church is indeed catholic. Its arms of compassion reach around the globe, bearing judgment against sin and offering mercy in reconciliation, disarming the powers of evil and unleashing the power of God, warning of the Day of Judgment and proclaiming the Day of the Lord. The language of the church's worship will openly manifest the church's concern for and bondage to the world God is creating and still loves.

Using Global Worship Resources

It is only natural that the liturgies of churches in the United States should reflect the culture of their Anglo-European ancestry—all peoples are influenced by the cultures in which they are born. So in traditional churches in the United States the music, architecture, speech, liturgical art, and worship styles are more closely connected to the Western than to the Eastern world and with classic Greek culture than with the cultures of Two-Thirds World nations. Even African American worship reflects more its North American than African cultural orientation, as, through the years, the prevailing Anglo-European culture has shaped African liturgical expressions, not only in the United States, but even in African countries.[6]

6. For example, Alex B. Chima ("Africanising the Liturgy: Where Are We Twenty

Moreover, through the years, the effort by Western Christianity to evangelize the nations of the world through various missionary movements was often characterized by identifying Christianity with Western culture, often idealized. Converts to Christianity were required to renounce native culture and religious practices and adapt to Western liturgical forms, worship styles, and institutional structures.[7] The historical record is that Anglo-European churches with great enthusiasm have commissioned their missionaries to carry liturgical expressions of their culture to Two-Thirds World countries but have been less enthusiastic about receiving cultural liturgical expressions from those countries. So cultural sharing between the church in the United States and Christians elsewhere around the globe has been largely a one-way street. Martin Marty has even proposed reversing the phrase "evangelize the world," which described an earlier generation's hope, to "en-world the evangel," a statement that he feels better summarizes the church's task now.[8]

But liturgies that reflect only their own native heritage and culture contradict the catholicity of the Christian church as well as deprive worshipers of the sheer joy of worshiping on multicultural levels. So it would be unfortunate if the worship of mainstream churches in the United States were to remain bound exclusively to unicultural liturgical language and forms. Robert Hovda gives this candid assessment of his own liturgical cultural conditioning:

> The author of this manual is a white, Anglo type, whose Norwegian g~ ndparents, Minnesota upbringing and seminary training (plus, no doubt, a lot of other things in the genes and in culture) conspired to inflate his estimation of cerebral values and to diminish his appreciation

---

Years After Vatican II?" *African Ecclesiastical Review* 25 [October 1983]: 286) argues that the post-Vatican Catholic church has done little to encourage genuinely African worship styles in the church in Africa: "The prayers composed and prescribed in Rome . . . despite their richness, belong to the Western world, and lack any African flavour." Robert E. Hood ("Can the Prayer Book Be Comprehensive for All Cultures?" *Anglican Theological Review* 66 [July 1984]: 280) contends that the Anglican Prayer Book "renders [black] culture and religious traditions either invisible or less worthy than a British/ North American white religious tradition," and should be supplemented with liturgical materials that reflect the integrity of the black culture.

7. See Leonel L. Mitchell, "At All Times and in All Places, or Each One in His or Her Own Place: Universality and/or Cultural Particularity in the Liturgy," *American Theological Library Association: Proceedings* 44 (June 1990): 100–110.

8. Marty, "Bonhoeffer," 469.

of many more fully human ones, to put it all too simply. I don't know quite how to explain the human diminishment I have too recently begun to feel—especially vis-à-vis black culture—except to say that, in comparison with it, I feel ill-at-ease in my body, stiff, inflexible, inhibited and somewhat constipated. Looking at problems of liturgical celebration in congregations predominantly of "my type" across this land, I do not believe I am unique or alone in suffering this kind of diminishment.[9]

One phenomenon of our present time is that individual nations in a large part of the world are rapidly becoming more and more polycultural, and that the fields of economics, politics, business, the arts, and athletics are losing some of their national exclusivity as they become more and more globally oriented. For example, the cover of Procter and Gamble Company's 1990 annual report carries a picture of children from six different nations, each holding a sample of the company's products. The report boasts that the company is now "truly [a] world company, a company that thinks of everything it does . . . in terms of the entire world."[10]

One might well question the motives behind the growing interest in globalization by multinational corporations, yet one can hardly question the reality that a new and widespread global consciousness is emerging in many quarters. William McElvaney, professor at Perkins School of Theology, comments: "To become globally conscious is actually to become aware of *what already is,* something like recognizing the law of gravity. . . . The interrelatedness and interdependence of the global neighborhood has become the common currency of our daily environment. Unless the church wants to become a dinosaur, we must be concerned to grow as global Christians and citizens."[11]

As Christ's body serving the world, the church will embrace a grand variety of liturgical expressions being prayed, sung, and spoken by

9. Robert W. Hovda, *Strong, Loving and Wise: Presiding in Liturgy* (Washington, D.C.: The Liturgical Conference, 1976), 31.

10. *The Proctor & Gamble Company 1990 Annual Report* (Cincinnati: The Procter & Gamble Company, 1990), 5.

11. William K. McElvaney, *Preaching from Camelot to Covenant: Announcing God's Action in the World* (Nashville: Abingdon Press, 1989), 78. Original emphasis. Robert E. Hood (*Must God Remain Greek? Afro Cultures and God-Talk* [Minneapolis: Fortress Press, 1991], xi) warns: "Despite its monumental contributions, the classical [Greek] legacy now threatens the survival and integrity of Christian identity in this world of many and varied cultures, where even fellow Christians bear far different assumptions than their Euro-American counterparts about what is good, beautiful, and even real."

136

Christians around the globe. In the United States, the use of litanies, responses, songs, creeds, and prayers from Latin America, Africa, Korea, and India, for example, challenges the cultural egocentricity that generally exists in worship liturgies by adding polycultural interest and a catholic perspective and, more important, by contributing a theological breadth and emotional energy not otherwise experienced. (See "Ecumenical and Global Liturgical Resources" in the Selected Resources at the end of this volume.) Images of God in African worship are vivid and down to earth: Source of All Life, Eternal Chief, Nursing Mother, Piler of Rocks into Towering Mountains, Rain, and Sun.[12] Native African prayers contain "not only an intrinsic beauty but a characteristically African style and urgency which is as redolent and evocative of authentic African worship as it is unfamiliar to the European."[13]

Already, through the writings of liberation theologians and pastors in Two-Thirds World churches, many clergy and laypersons in One-Third World countries have been awakened to fresh interpretations of scripture, sensitized to the interrelatedness of liturgy and justice, and drawn into the struggles of the powerless. Sharing in the liturgies of minority nations embodies in the church's worship something of the unity for which Christ prayed. It enriches, enlarges, and enlivens native concepts of God as it expands parochial views of the church's mission.[14] In the section that follows, we will review an assortment of native liturgical expressions originating in congregations of widely divergent cultures.

Beginning of Worship

Traditionally, the Invitation to Worship, or Opening Sentences, in most liturgies in English-speaking countries is either a biblical text or is based on a biblical text. In Two-Thirds World countries, though, worship often begins with extrabiblical materials. Here is a Call to Worship written in extrabiblical language from Cameroon, West Africa, that communicates the drama and energy of worship and anticipates its promise:

12. Joseph G. Healey, "Indigenization: Africa," in J. G. Davies, *The New Westminster Dictionary of Liturgy and Worship* (Philadelphia: Westminster Press, 1986), 270.

13. Anthony Gittins, *Heart of Prayer: African, Jewish and Biblical Prayers* (London: Collins Liturgical Publications, 1985), 10.

14. See McElvaney, *Camelot to Covenant*, 84, esp. 77–91.

Leader: It is Sunday! It is Sunday!

People: Get awake! Don't sit down!
Come to this good thing that won't come to you unless you come to it!

Leader: Come to Sunday meeting, everybody!

People: Come all! Don't just sit in your town today!

Leader: The words of God have arrived! Come and hear them!

People: No one else can hear them for you!
You must come!
It is Sunday! Sunday![15]

In the Invitation to Worship below, from a poem by Elsa Tamez of Costa Rica, the eucharistic references are rendered in striking imagery:

Leader: Come, O people, come!

People: Let us celebrate the supper of the Lord,
let us together break a giant loaf
and together prepare the jars of wine
as at the wedding feast in Cana.

Leader: Come, O people, come to the table of the Lord.

People: Let the women not forget the salt
nor the men the leaven
and let us invite many guests:
the lame, the blind, the deaf, the poor.

Leader: Come, O people, come for this meeting with the Lord.

People: Quickly, now!
Let us follow the recipe of the Lord:
Let us together knead the dough with our hands,
and watch with joy the rising bread.

Leader: Come, O people, come, for this celebration with our Lord.

People: Because today we are celebrating
our commitment to Christ Jesus;
today we are renewing our commitment to the kingdom;
and no one shall go hungry away.

15. From the author's collection. Source unknown.

Leader: Come, let us participate in the feast of life with our Lord.[16]

The first part of this prayer from a Dakota tribe could serve as an opening prayer for worship:

> Grandfather, Great Spirit, you have always been, and before you nothing has been. There is no one to pray to but you. The star nations all over the heavens are yours, and yours are the grasses of the earth. You are older than all need, older than all pain and prayer.
>
> Grandfather, Great Spirit, all over the world the faces of living ones are alike. With tenderness they have come up out of the ground. Look upon your children, with children in their arms, that they may face the winds and walk the good road to the day of quiet.

The concluding part of the prayer is appropriate for the close of worship:

> Grandfather, Great Spirit, fill us with the light. Give us the strength to understand and eyes to see. Teach us to walk the soft earth as relatives to all that live.[17]

The three brief prayers below come from new Christian converts in Haiti. They invite people to worship and are built around metaphors of everyday experience:

> Lord, we have come to Your marketplace.
> We know there are plenty of provisions in Your market.
> We have brought our baskets with us; and now we want to go back
>   from Your market
> With our baskets full of provisions.[18]

> Jesus, Your words are to us as a mirror,
>   a bath, a powdering and perfuming.
> Then help us to rise up with a fresh [bath]
> And go out among the world this week.[19]

> [Lord,] this morning the preacher will
>   distribute Your Word

16. *Jesus Christ—the Life of the World: Prayers and Litanies* (Geneva: World Council of Churches, 1983), 69–70.

17. Justo and Catherine González, *In Accord: Let Us Worship* (New York: Friendship Press, 1981), 63.

18. Sandra L. Burdick, ed., *God Is No Stranger* (Grand Rapids, Mich.: Baptist Haiti Mission, 1970).

19. Burdick, *Stranger.*

Without ration cards.[20]

This Invitation to Worship incorporates a prayer from Cameroon, Sierra Leone, Uganda, that uses traditional names for God, each of which denotes a characteristic of deity:

Leader: To name God is to call forth God's presence in our midst and to speak the love that bonds humanity together. Let us, therefore, call the names of God, bind ourselves to our sisters and brothers in Africa, and invite the Giver of all life to be with us as we pray and share in this time of worship.

All: God, you are the RUHANGA (*Roo-HANG-uh*), the Creator.

God, you are MEBEE (*ME-bee*), the One who gives birth to the world.

God, you are RUTUNGABORO (*Roo-TUNG-uh-bor-uh*), the Protector of the poor.

God, you are MEKETA (*Meh-KEY-tuh*), the everlasting One. Amen.[21]

Eucharistic Prayers

The poem "The Good Mass" by Costa Rican Jorge Debravo, could serve effectively either as an Invitation to Worship or as a prayer before the Eucharist:

Let us celebrate
the Mass of love this morning.
We shall make a host
of corn meal, flour, and hope.
On a rocky ledge,
in the bowels of a hill,
we shall consecrate the host of life
and the wine of right.

. . . .

We shall all be priests, all,
the high and low.
And we shall all eat the host of love

---

20. Burdick, *Stranger*.

21. Gary P. Davidson, ed., *Banquet of Praise* (Washington, D.C.: Bread for the World, 1990), 8.

like warm animals.
We shall invite everyone to the Mass:
children, the aged, prisoners,
pilots and mechanics,
archbishops and laborers.[22]

Two of the liturgical poems of Samuel Rayan of India are appropriate
for use in a eucharistic celebration, the first as an invitation to the
table, the second as a response afterwards:

13.
jesus continues to eat with us.
he may be our guest and we his any day
in our bastis, barrios, favelas, and inner-city slums.
kosuke koyama, japanese theologian, tells us of his experiences:
    dear friends,
    we had rice with jesus!
    the place was tondo, cebu, central luzon.
    our menu was dried fish, some strange soup, and rice.
    he looked to us as though he was indignant.
    he looked to us as though he was infinitely concerned.
    he looked to us as though . . . [pause].
let us pray:
give us this day our daily bread.

21.
say,
sing,
dance
the lord's prayer together,
so that all of us may become a loaf of bread broken
and a bowl or rice shared
for the revelation of god
and the life of the world.[23]

Thanksgivings

In a Prayer of Thanksgiving by Rubem Alves of Brazil, even though
the names of some fruits and flowers are in Spanish, the sounds of

22. Hugo Assmann, "The Faith of the Poor in Their Struggle with Idols," in Pablo
Richard et al., *The Idols of Death and the God of Life* (Maryknoll, N.Y.: Orbis Books,
1983), 226.
23. Sergio Torres and John Eagleson, eds., *The Challenge of Basic Christian Communities* (Maryknoll, N.Y.: Orbis Books, 1981), 223, 227.

the words themselves help create mental images of tropical colors and shapes, even for those who may not know the language:

> Help us to sense [or: We thank you for]
> the beauty and the dignity of our bodies:
> the caresses of persons, of animals, or nature;
> the good taste of food;
> the smell of lush grass, of jasmine, of beans;
> the sound of the wind in the leaves of the trees,
> the noise of the ocean, the streams that play tag with the rocks,
> the berimbau, the organs, the drums, the laughter;
> the body with gooseflesh in cold wind;
> the taste of the jaboticaba fruit, or the grapes, the mangos;
> the blue of the sea, the yellow of the ipe trees,
> the green of the pau-ferro bushes, the red of the parrots;
> the capacity to play, cook, plant, walk, enjoy laziness in the hammock,
> in the blessing of your rest, which bids us do nothing,
> and to receive the grace of life, the power to love.[24]

Here is a simple prayer by Ghanaian fishermen that expresses an exuberant thanksgiving for a divine blessing in language that is nonsentimental and surprisingly direct for non-Africans:

> We have drawn them in,
> Stamping the rhythm with our feet, the muscles tense.
> We have sung your praise.
> On the beach, there were our mammies,
> Who bought the blessing out of the nets,
> Out of the nets into their basins.
> They rushed to the market, returned and bought again.
> Lord, what a blessing is the sea with fish in plenty!
> Lord, that is the story of your grace.
> Nets tear, and we succumb because we cannot hold them![25]

In the Tamil form of worship as prepared by the Tamilnadu Theological Seminary in Arasaradi, Madurai, India, the traditional "Mangalam" is sung.[26] It might also serve as a spoken doxology:

> Blessed be the great Lord Jesus, the Lord One and Three,

---

24. Rubem Alves, *I Believe in the Resurrection of the Body* (Philadelphia: Fortress Press, 1986), 58.

25. Aylward Shorter, *Prayer in the Religious Traditions of Africa* (New York: Oxford University Press, 1975), 82.

26. " 'Mangalam' is a word of blessing that expresses the welling-up of joy on the part of the person who says or sings the blessing. The person to whom mangalam is addressed will be the object of fond devotion and will be showered with sayings of

eternal, savior of the world, teacher, musician,
infinite, alpha, lover, omnipresent,
lover of justice, supreme child, everlasting virtue,
helper, and God with us.[27]

Response to the Reading of Scripture

In some communions the congregation participates in brief responses made before and after the reading of scripture lessons. In a liturgy from Zaire, this exchange between reader and congregation takes place before the Gospel lesson is read:

Reader: Brothers and sisters: the Word was made flesh,

People: And he dwelled among us.

Reader: Let us listen to him.

Following the reading there is this exchange:

Reader: The Good News, as Saint [Name] has written it.

People: Announce it, announce it, we are listening.

Then, following the sermon:

Reader: He who has ears to hear

People: Let him hear!

Reader: He who has a heart to receive

People: Let him receive![28]

Confessions

Prayers originating in Two-Thirds World countries, especially in places where the poor are oppressed and face acts of injustice from the ruling elite, often contribute historical relevance to our prayers of confession, expressing the scope of human sinfulness in ways that

blessings and praises" (*Worship Through Tamil Music* [Arasarai, Madurai: Tamilnadu Theological Seminary Press, n.d.], 14).

27. *Tamil Music,* 14.

28. Max Thurian and Geoffrey Wainwright, eds., *Baptism and Eucharist: Ecumenical Convergence in Celebration* (Grand Rapids, Mich.: Wm. B. Eerdmans, 1983), 206.

prayers in traditional One-Third World churches do not. This one is from South America:

> *Lord, when did we see you?*
> I was hungry and starving
>   and you were obese;
> Thirsty
>   and you were watering your garden;
> With no road to follow, and without hope
>   and you called the police and were
>   happy that they took me prisoner;
> Barefoot and with ragged clothing
>   and you were saying "I have nothing
>   to wear, tomorrow I will buy something new";
> Sick
>   and you asked: "Is it infectious?"
> Prisoner
>   and you said: "That is where all those
>   of your class should be";
> Lord, have mercy![29]

The confession below, prepared by the Aikya Group in Bangalore, India, although extremely personal, communicates a deep sorrow for sin, using such graphic metaphors as a hurricane and a rejected lover:

> I have fallen, Lord, once more.
> I can't go on, I'll never succeed.
> I am ashamed, I don't dare look at you.
> And yet I struggled, Lord, for I knew you were right near me,
>   bending over me, watching.
> But temptation blew like a hurricane
> And instead of looking at you I turned my head away,
> I stepped aside while you stood, silent and sorrowful,
> Like the spurned fiance who sees his loved one
>   carried off by his rival.
>
> I'm so ashamed that I feel like crawling to avoid being seen,
> I'm ashamed of being seen by my friend,
> I'm ashamed of being seen by you, Lord,
> For you loved me, and I forgot you.
> I forgot you because I was thinking of myself,
> And one can't think of several persons at once.
> One must choose, and I chose.[30]

This confession from India is similar:

29. *For All God's People: Ecumenical Prayer Cycle* (Geneva: World Council of Churches, 1978), 193.

30. Roger Ortmayer, ed., *Sing and Pray and Shout Hurray* (New York: Friendship Press, 1974), 25.

Like an ant on a stick both ends of which are burning,
   I go to and from without knowing what to do,
   and in great despair,
Like the inescapable shadows that follow me,
   the dead weight of sin haunts me.
Graciously look upon me.
Thy love is my refuge. Amen.[31]

The confessional below is translated and adapted from the Spanish:

Because we have seen pain without being moved,
because we forget your love with solemn pride,
because we pass by happy before poverty and sadness,
Lord have mercy on us.
For speaking of love without loving our sister or brother,
for speaking of faith without living your word,
because we live without seeing our personal evil, our sin,
Christ have mercy on us.
For our tranquility in our affluent life,
for our great falseness in preaching about poverty,
for wanting to make excuses for injustice and misery,
Lord have mercy on us.[32]

Here is a simple confession built around an experience of a new Christian convert in Haiti:

Lord, we are like the lady
   Madame Wallace took to the Psychiatric Center.
The lady had lost some pages from her book.
We, too, seem to have lost some pages.
   We are unregenerate. So we come to You
So You can put us back in the Way.[33]

Intercessions

Prayer intercessions from Two-Thirds World countries often represent conditions and social realities not found in the prayers of developed

---

31. *The United Methodist Hymnal* (Nashville: United Methodist Publishing House, 1989), 535.

32. *Book of Worship: United Church of Christ* (New York: United Church of Christ Office for Church Life and Leadership, 1986), 532–33.

33. Burdick, *Strangers.*

nations. They can reflect the hostile and tense relationships that sometimes exist between different social classes, as this prayer does from
the Evangelical Church of the River Plate, Argentina:

> We pray for those who govern.
> Teach them that You are the ruler of all
> and that they are only Your instruments.
> Grant them wisdom for their difficult decisions,
> a sharp eye for what is essential,
> and courage to obey Your commandment.
>
> We pray for all who continue to seek salvation in violence.
> Show terrorists that no blessing rests on violence.
> Take the young among them especially into Your care
> and bring order into their confused thoughts.
> Bring murder and kidnapping to an end.
>
> We pray for all judges
> that they may pronounce just decisions;
> for all prisoners
> that they may make good use of their time of imprisonment;
> for all their warders
> that they may not run out of patience.
>
> We pray for all refugees.
> Grant that they may soon find a home again.
> We pray for the people who have disappeared
> and for their relatives.
> Deliver parents and children, husband and wife
> from torturing uncertainty.
>
> We pray for all who are no longer able to sleep in peace
> because they fear [for] their own life
> and for that of those near and dear to them;
> we pray for all who no longer hope in Your Kingdom;
> for all who are tormented by anxiety or despair.
> Grant that they may be blessed
> with faithful friends and counsellors alongside them
> to comfort them with Your strengthening Gospel and Sacrament.
>
> Lord, You have the whole wide world in Your hands;
> You are able to turn human hearts as seems best to You;
> grant Your grace therefore to the bonds of peace and love,
> and in all lands join together whatever has been torn asunder.[34]

34. Hans-Georg Link, ed., *Confessing Our Faith Around the World* (Geneva: World
Council of Churches, 1983), 4:10–11.

The intercessions that follow are taken from a paraphrase of The Lord's Prayer in a liturgy from Nicaragua:

Grant us strength that, in this our native land,
we may be able to build a society in which all
have enough to eat,
a roof over their heads, and schools for their children,
safety and peace;
a society in which soon we shall be able to turn swords into
    ploughshares
and tanks to instruments for useful toil;
a society which is new, with new women and new men
who delight more in giving
than in receiving.

Lead us not into the temptation to think ourselves already straight,
good Christians already on the right road.
Let us not be tempted
into pride at what we have already achieved or
into despair at all that is still required.
Lead us not into the temptation
of morosity, routine, or hatred.[35]

Brazilian Rubem Alves includes these petitions in one of his prayers:

May these sacramental gifts make us remember those who do not receive
    them:
who have their lives cut every day, in the bread absent from the table;
in the door of the hospital, the prison, the welfare home that does not
    open;
in sad children, feet without shoes, eyes without hope;
in war hymns that glorify death;
in deserts where once there was life.[36]

Dedications of Life

From India comes this liturgy of "Surrender and Dedication," which could serve either as a personal or collective prayer of commitment, perhaps after the sermon or in a service of baptism renewal:

35. Link, *Confessing Our Faith*, 3:57–58.
36. *United Methodist Hymnal*, 639.

Me, I surrender as a living sacrifice;
Do accept me, Jesus.
My mother and father, standing in thy presence
    had made promises.
This apart, I now dedicate myself.
From the darkness and from the slavery of the sinful devil,
Father, thou, with thy blood as a price, delivered me.
To you I surrender myself.
My soul and body, to thee I present that thou take it for a vessel.
I wait. Be gracious to me, O Lord!
As an instrument of justice, I place myself at your disposal,
That it may be the temple of the Holy Spirit.
I present my body as your own.[37]

Confessions of Faith

Confessions of faith, or creeds, from communions in other nations often express perceptions of the Christian faith that can enrich traditional statements. This one, a proposed Confession of Faith for the church in Southern Africa, firmly voices the connection of the Christian faith to social justice, an interest that is missing from the traditional creeds, and even from most contemporary confessions in mainstream churches in the United States:

I believe in Jesus Christ,
    who came, in the authority of God, to share our misery,
    who voluntarily became the victim of our enmity against our Creator
    to redeem us from sin, evil, and death,
    from oppression and exploitation,
    from greed and craving for power,
    from hatred and suspicion,
    from self-aggrandizement and arbitrariness,
    from our fear of each other and of the future,
    from our enslavement by drugs and sorcery,
    by prejudice and traditions that separate us,
    by ideologies of race, class, ethnicity or family,
    by detrimental programmes and static structures.
Who rose from the dead
    to endow us all with his new life,
    a life in freedom and joy,
    a life in brotherly love,
    a life in common service to the benefit of all,

---

37. *Tamil Music,* 12–13.

a life struggling against poverty and injustice,
against sickness and ignorance,
a life in responsibility for those that will
come after us and inhabit our land
a life which witnesses to his salvation in word and deed,
a life assured of his rule,
a life of hope in his future for us all.[38]

In a similar way, the Creed from South Africa clearly unites Christian belief with commitment to social justice, yet in language that is quite different from the statement above:

Jesus has taught us to speak of hope as the coming of God's Kingdom.
We believe that God is at work in our world turning hopeless and evil situations into good.
We believe that goodness and justice and love will triumph in the end, and that tyranny and oppression cannot last forever.
One day "all tears will be wiped away" and "the lamb will lie down with the lion."
True peace and true reconciliation are not only desirable, they are assured and guaranteed.
This is our faith, and our hope.[39]

Because creedal statements and confessions of faith vary considerably among churches of any nation or culture, contemporary statements such as the two above may not always be fully acceptable, as written, in some communions. Is it permissible to alter or adapt such statements to make them more suitable for a particular church's use? Because these are contemporary statements and not the historic creeds of the church, it would seem that, in most instances, careful editing and adapting of the statements would be permissible—at least under certain conditions: for example, providing that the original meaning and intention were not substantially altered, and that the changes made were clearly indicated. However, the value of using multicultural liturgical materials depends largely upon their unique linguistic expressions and theological orientation; making them culturally palatable would likely reduce, if not remove, their unique contributions.

38. John de Gruchy, ed., *Cry Justice: Prayers, Meditations, and Readings from South Africa* (Maryknoll, N.Y.: Orbis Books, 1986), 90–91.
39. *Third World Solidarity Day* (Toronto: Canadian Catholic Organization for Development and Peace, 1987), 24.

I believe in God, the Creator of all things and Maker of all [persons], yet who does not reign according to unchangeable laws, or will that inequalities and injustice should remain.

I believe in God, the Great Subversive Agent on behalf of the poor and needy, who sustains us to live for the Creation of a new society.

I believe in Jesus Christ, who shared and responded creatively to every part of our human experience and was crucified at an age when today he would have been too young for important work in the church.

I believe in Jesus Christ, who through his obedience to the Father, the intensity of his love for others and his resurrection after death, unites in one personality all those who obey his call.

I believe in the Holy Spirit, who gives men and women the strength to do what is just and right, and gives to the unending cosmic dimension every act of service and compassion.

I believe in the Holy Spirit, who helps us selfish individuals to transcend the barriers of ethnic, racial, cultural and linguistic differences, and unites us as a single fellowship.[40]

A Nicaraguan "Peasant Creed":

I believe in You: architect, engineer, artisan and
carpenter, mason and shipbuilder . . .
I believe in You: the laborer Christ—light of light, and
truly firstborn Son of God,
Who to save the world took human flesh in the pure and
humble womb of Mary.
I believe that you were scourged, mocked, and tortured,
Martyred on the cross by the praetorian Pilate—
That imperialist Roman, merciless and cruel.
He washed his hands, trying to erase his mistake.
I believe in You, who walk with me by the way—
The human Christ, the worker-Christ, who conquered death.
Your tremendous sacrifice gave birth to a new man
And began his liberation . . .[41]

A creed from the French Reformed church:

We believe in God . . .
Despite his being silent and hidden,
we believe that he is alive.
Despite the existence of evil and suffering,
we believe that he has made the world for happiness and life.

40. The Aikya Group of Bangalore, India, in Ortmayer, *Sing and Pray,* 24–25.
41. Guillermo Cook, *The Expectation of the Poor* (Maryknoll, N.Y.: Orbis Books, 1985), 120.

Despite the limits of our minds and the rebellion of our hearts,
  we believe in God.

We believe in Jesus Christ . . .
Despite the centuries separating us from him,
  we believe in his word.
Despite his weakness and poverty,
  we believe that his death is our life.
Despite our lack of understanding and our failure,
  we believe that he is risen.

We believe in the Holy Spirit . . .
Despite appearances,
  we believe that he guides the Church.
Despite death,
  we believe in resurrection.
Despite the existence of ignorance and unbelief,
  we believe that the kingdom of God is for all people everywhere.[42]

Hymnody

If, as the popular saying puts it, music is "an international language,"
then singing the hymns of Christians in other countries should be a
chief means of experiencing inclusive, polycultural worship. Until
recently, locating multinational hymns for supplemental use by
churches in the United States required extensive research—the popular
church hymnbooks contained few, if any, such hymns. Some of the
recently published hymnals, though, include an impressive number
of ethnic hymns, providing the church with alternative images and
theological perspectives. For example, the Latin American carol "A
La Ru" ("O Sleep, Dear Holy Baby") portrays the manger scene with
dramatic plainness, through the mother's expressions of love and the
simple folk melody:

O sleep, dear holy Baby,
with Your head against my breast;
meanwhile the pangs of my sorrow
are soothed and put to rest.

You need not fear King Herod,
he will bring no harm to You;
so rest in the arms of Your mother,
who sings You a la ru.

42. Link, *Confessing Our Faith*, 2:46.

A la ru, a la mé,
a la ru, a la mé,
a la ru, a la mé,
a la ru, a la ru, a la mé.[43]

The *Psalter Hymnal*,[44] *The United Methodist Hymnal*, and *The Presbyterian Hymnal: Hymns, Psalms, and Spiritual Songs*, in particular, have included a variety of hymnody deriving from non-European cultures, most of which have been translated into English, but some in their native language: by my count, the United Methodist hymnal contains thirty, the Presbyterian hymnal, twenty-nine, and the *Psalter Hymnal*, twenty-three. The United Methodist and the Presbyterian hymnals include a version of "Amazing Grace" with stanzas written in five Native American dialects.

Although some hymns written in native tongues may be difficult for congregations to sing (hymns in Spanish usually require practice) others are quite singable. For example, this hymn, written in a Native American dialect, could be sung by most congregations with a minimum of practice:

Wo-ta-nin was-te na-hon po, Je-sus he wa-ih-dus-na:
Hear the good news of salvation: Jesus died to show God's love.
To-wa-o-si-da kin tan-ka, He de-han i-yo-ma-hi.
Such great kindness! Such great mercy! Come to us from heaven above.
Je-sus Christ was-tee-wa-da-ka, Je-sus Christ ni-ma-y-an:
Jesus Christ, how much I love You! Jesus Christ, You save from sin!
Han, was-tewa-dake am-at-on-wa, Is eya was-te-ma-da.
How I love You! Look upon me. Love me still and cleanse within.[45]

If the native tongue of a hymn is too complicated for congregational singing, the refrain alone might be sung in the original language, the stanzas in English. The stanzas of the Spanish hymn "Alleluia" ("Alabaré") describe the singing of the saints in heaven before the throne of the Lamb, while the refrain is the words of the song they sing:

A-la-ba-ré, a-la-ba-ré, a-la-ba-ré a mi Se-ñor.
A-la-ba-ré, a-la-ba-ré, a-la-ba-ré a mi Se-ñor.[46]

---

43. *The Presbyterian Hymnal: Hymns, Psalms, and Spiritual Songs* (Louisville: Westminster/John Knox, 1990), 45.

44. *Psalter Hymnal* (Grand Rapids, Mich.: Christian Reformed Church Publications, 1987).

45. *Presbyterian Hymnal*, 355.

46. *Psalter Hymnal*, 234.

In the "Great Hymn" from Xhosa, Africa, a similar arrangement makes the African dialect singable:

Stanza:
It is you are the Great God, who dwells on high,
It is you, it is you, true shield, protector,
It is you, it is you, true fortress, stronghold,
It is you, it is you, true forest of refuge,
It is you, it is you, true rock of power,
It is you, it is you, who dwells in the highest.

Refrain:
Ele le le homna, hom, homna
Ele le le homna, hom, homna
Ele le le homna, hom, homna.[47]

Similarly, although the words of the Pakistani hymn "Saranam, Saranam" are mostly in English, the native word *Saranam* ("refuge") is repeated frequently. The hymn is sung to a traditional Punjabi melody:

Stanza:
In the midst of foes I cry to thee,
from the ends of earth wherever I may be;
my strength in helplessness, O answer me:
Saranam, Saranam, Saranam.

Refrain:
Jesus, Savior, Lord, lo, to thee I fly:
Saranam, Saranam, Saranam;
thou the Rock, my refuge that's higher than I:
Saranam, Saranam, Saranam.[48]

Reading and Interpreting Scripture

Some congregations in the United States have members who can read or speak a foreign language. These persons might be used periodically (or on special Sundays such as World Missions, Pentecost, or Worldwide Communion Sunday) to read the scripture lessons in one or more different languages. Some congregations learn to say the Lord's Prayer or one of the creeds in a foreign language, or say them in several

47. De Gruchy, *Cry Justice*, 58.
48. *United Methodist Hymnal*, 523.

languages at once.[49] The sound of another language itself serves to remind worshipers of their membership in a world community, and that the gospel "belongs" not to any single nation or culture, but to the whole world. William McElvaney says that, in his experience, when another language is used in liturgy, "the whole service takes on a new dimension, a quality of universality, yet infinite particularity, a sense of the majesty of God, the wonder of cultural differences and a global faith community. . . . It is the fact that I do *not* understand what is being said that lends an air of mystery, gift, and challenge, a shifting into a transcendent and global gear."[50]

One of the most valuable commentaries a preacher can have is *The Gospel in Solentiname*, by Ernesto Cardinal.[51] The volumes consist of comments and reflections on various Gospel texts made by campesinos of Solentiname, a remote archipelago on Lake Nicaragua. Under the leadership of Father Cardinal, each Sunday at Mass the community of Our Lady of Solentiname, instead of having a sermon on the Gospel reading, holds a dialogue. The volumes are a collection of those dialogues, recorded as they were spoken and including the speakers' names. These might be used in a worship liturgy in various ways: as a congregational response to the Gospel lesson, as a part of the sermon (or *as* the sermon), or as a congregational response to the sermon. The various speaking parts can be read by representative members of the assembly, or they can be put into the form of a litany or responsive reading. For example, after the reading of the Matthean text, "You are the salt of the earth" (5:13), persons selected from the congregation might read this dialogue:

> Adán: It seems to me it's because every meal should have salt. A meal without salt has no taste. We must give taste to the world.
> Julio: By liberating it. Because a world filled with injustice is tasteless. Mainly for the poor, life like that has no taste.
> Marcelino: You only need a little salt, because it's strong. You add just a tiny bit. There are only a few of us, but we can give taste to the world.
> Doña Adela, a little old woman with a weak voice: We are the salt of the world because we have been placed in it so the world won't rot.

49. The *Presbyterian Hymnal* contains the Apostles' Creed and the Lord's Prayer in English, Spanish, and Korean.

50. McElvaney, *Camelot to Covenant*, 83–84.

51. Ernesto Cardenal, *The Gospel in Solentiname*, trans. Donald T. Marsh, 4 vols. (Maryknoll, N.Y.: Orbis Books, 1976).

. . . .

Olivia: It seems to me that the salt has got lost when instead of preserving justice on earth, Christians have let injustice multiply more, as has happened now in capitalist society. We Christians wanted to prevent that, but we haven't. Instead, Christians have sided with injustice, with capitalism. We have sided with selfishness. We have been useless salt.

Felipe: Christianity that stopped being Christian, that's the salt that doesn't salt any more.

Laureano: Christianity that stopped being revolutionary, that lost its taste.

. . . . . .

Marcelino: I think that "salt" is the Gospel word given to us so that we'll practice it and pass it on to others, practicing love, so that everybody will have it. Because salt is a thing that you never deny to anybody. When somebody is very stingy they say that "he wouldn't give you salt for a sour prune." That's why Jesus says "have salt," which means to have love shared out among everybody, and so we'll have everything shared out, we'll all be equal and we'll live united and in peace.

Pancho: Doesn't it probably mean that in spite of sin and injustice, which have always got to exist, and in spite of the salt or bad luck that is our lot, we must live in peace with one another, rich and poor?

. . . . . .

Olivia: It's all the same, "have love," "have salt."

Manuel: Yes, because anyone who doesn't have salt is sick.[52]

The use of this kind of commentary from Christian sisters and brothers in Central America brings inclusiveness of language and culture into the liturgies of North American congregations in intensive and dramatic ways: it is, in effect, as if neighbor were sitting down with neighbor, participating in the worship, interpreting God's Word.

Close of Worship

This prayer from India is appropriate for use either at the beginning of worship, anticipating the divine presence in the service, or at the end of worship, anticipating a witness to God in the world:

As you have set the moon in the sky to be the poor man's lantern,
so let your Light shine in our dark lives and lighten our paths;
as the rice is sown in the water and brings forth grain in great abundance,
so let your Word be sown in our midst that the harvest may be great;

52. Cardenal, *Gospel,* 1:190–93, passim.

and as the banyan sends forth its branches to take root in the soil,
so let your Life take root in our lives.[53]

The litany below is based on a prayer from the Dinka congregation
in Sudan:

Leader: In the time when God created all things, God created the
sun and the moon.

People: We praise you, O Lord!

Leader: God created the stars.

People: We praise you, O Lord!

Leader: God created the earth and all living things.

People: We praise you, O Lord!

Leader: God created humanity.

People: In God's own image humanity was made.

Leader: Never to be hungry or thirsty.

People: But to live with the fullness of life.

Leader: In God's vision of a new heaven and a new earth.

People: Indeed, this is GOOD NEWS!

Leader: We go forth to tell the nations.

People: Thanks be to God![54]

A group of Native American women prepared a liturgy for the World
Day of Prayer, 6 March 1981, for Church Women United, which
included this Dismissal:

Now Talking God,
With your feet I walk,
I walk with your limbs,
I carry forth your body,
For me your mind thinks,
Your voice speaks for me.
Beauty is before me
And beauty behind me.
Above and below me hovers the beautiful,
I am surrounded by it,

53. George Appleton, ed., *The Oxford Book of Prayer* (New York: Oxford University
Press, 1985), 298. The prayer has been adapted using the plural.
54. Davidson, *Banquet of Praise*, 70.

I am immersed in it.
In my youth I am aware of it,
And in old age
I shall walk quietly
The beautiful trail.[55]

Some of the liturgical prayers offered by Christians in Samburu, Kenya, will include, at the end, the divine answer the worshipers can expect to receive: "And God said: 'All right!' " as in this prayer, adapted here for use as a dismissal:

My God, you will save us.
My God, you will guide us.
Make us live long like a dark cloud—the long rains.
Make us fragrant like a citron branch that purifies.
God, guard us.
My God, who are surrounded with stars,
with the moon at your navel,
morning of my God that will rise,
hit us with a blessed wind.
Flood us with your waters.
And God said: "All right!"[56]

Because God has placed the church in the world to serve as the body of Christ, God also has conferred upon the church the Holy Spirit to empower it to do the work of Christ. So the church's work cannot be done selectively. It cannot discriminate among whom or for whom its ministry will be, because to do so would be to violate its nature to practice the all-inclusive love of its Lord.

Because the language of the church is a form of sacred speech, and because words do not merely communicate sounds but also power, the language of the church's liturgy will be inclusive: it will not favor predominating persons or groups, it will not respect the preferences or status systems of secular society, and it will not exclude the unpopular, unseemly, or disliked. Rather, in the language of its prayers of intercession, in its thanksgivings and confessions, in its preaching and even in its singing and reading of scripture, the church will speak transculturally, bearing witness to the all-encompassing love of Jesus Christ for the whole world. Whether intended or not, exclusive or

---

55. Justo and Catherine González, *In Accord*, 41.
56. Gittins, *Heart of Prayer*, 114.

unicultural liturgical speech communicates an indifference by the church toward the world it is meant to serve. But whenever worshiping Christians speak their liturgies in the language of their Lord, embracing all human classes and types and nationalities as family members, then they are engaging themselves with the realities of their history. Then they are joining their voices with the witness of Doña Adela of So-lentiname, the "little old woman with a weak voice," in saying: "We are the salt of the world because we have been placed in it so the world won't rot."[57]

57. Cardenal, *Gospel,* 1:193.

Selected Resources

Worshipbooks and Worship Resources

Blessings and Consecrations: A Book of Occasional Services. Nashville: Abingdon Press, 1984.

Book of Common Prayer: Episcopal Church. New York: Seabury Press, 1979.

Book of Services. Nashville: United Methodist Church Publishing House, 1985.

The Book of Worship of the African Methodist Episcopal Church. Nashville: A.M.E. Sunday School Union, 1984.

Book of Worship: United Church of Christ. New York: United Church of Christ Office for Church Life and Leadership, 1986.

Confession of Faith and Directory for Worship for Cumberland Presbyterians. Memphis: Frontier Press, 1984.

Duck, Ruth C., and Maren C. Tirabassi, eds. *Touch Holiness: Resources for Worship.* New York: Pilgrim Press, 1990.

Emswiler, Sharon Neufer, and Thomas Emswiler. *Sisters and Brothers, Sing!* Normal, Ill.: Wesley Foundation, 1977. Includes 133 new and traditional hymns written primarily for youth. Order from: The Wesley Foundation, 211 North School St., Normal, IL 61761.

Emswiler, Sharon Neufer, and Thomas Emswiler. *Wholeness in Worship: Creative Models for Sunday, Family and Special Services.* San Francisco: Harper & Row, 1980.

Emswiler, Sharon Neufer, and Thomas Emswiler. *Women and Worship: A Guide to Hymns, Prayers, and Liturgies.* San Francisco: Harper & Row, 1984.

Gjerding, Iben, and Katharine Kinnamon, eds. *No Longer Strangers: A Resource for Women and Worship.* Nashville: Abingdon Press, 1984.

Hamma, Robert, ed. *Still More Children's Liturgies.* New York: Paulist Press, 1990.

159

SELECTED RESOURCES

Hickman, Hoyt L., et al. *Handbook of the Christian Year*. Nashville: Abingdon Press, 1986.

Holy Communion: A Service Book for Use by the Minister. Nashville: United Methodist Church, 1987.

Huck, Gabe, ed. *The Liturgy Documents*. 2d ed. Chicago: Liturgy Training Publications, 1985.

———, ed. *Simple Gifts: A Collection of Ideas and Rites for Liturgy*. 2 vols. Washington, D.C.: Liturgical Conference, 1974.

Jesus Christ—the Life of the World: Prayers and Litanies. New York: World Council of Churches, 1983.

Liturgy Training Series. Chicago: Liturgy Training Publications:
A Christmas Sourcebook, 1984.
Parish Path through Advent and Christmastide, 1983.
Parish Path through Lent and Eastertide, 2d ed. 1985.
The Three Days: Parish Prayers in the Paschal Triduum, 1981.
A Triduum Sourcebook, 1983.

Lutheran Book of Worship. Minneapolis: Augsburg, 1976.

Mitman, F. Russell. *Worship Vessels: Resources for Renewal*. San Francisco: Harper & Row, 1986.

O'Day, Rey. *Theatre of the Spirit: A Worship Handbook*. New York: Pilgrim Press, 1980.

Rainsley, Glen E. *Words of Worship: Resources for Church and Home*. New York: Pilgrim Press, 1991.

The Rites of the Catholic Church. 2 vols. New York: Pueblo Publishing, 1983.

Schwartz, Faye, and David Mohr. *Creative Worship*. Lima, Oh.: C.S.S. Publishing Co., 1982.

The Service for the Lord's Day: The Worship of God. Philadelphia: Westminster Press, 1984.

We Gather Together: Services of Public Worship. Nashville: Abingdon Press, 1980.

Winter, Miriam Therese. *WomanPrayer, WomanSong: Resources for Ritual*. Oak Park, Ill.: Meyer-Stone Books, 1987.

———. *WomanWorld: A Feminist Lectionary and Psalter*. New York: Crossroad/Continuum, 1990.

Worship the Lord: Reformed Church in America. Grand Rapids, Mich.: Wm. B. Eerdmans, 1987.

Ecumenical and Global Liturgical Resources

Banquet of Praise. Washington, D.C.: Bread for the World, 1990. Hymns, songs, prayers, collects, and readings that focus on hunger, peace, and justice, in a broad spectrum of denominational and cultural traditions. Inclusive language throughout. Order from: 802 Rhode Island Avenue, NE, Washington, DC 20002.

Book of Worship: United Church of Christ. New York: United Church of Christ Office for Church Life and Leadership, 1986. Several multicultural resources are included in the back of the worshipbook under "Resources."

Burdick, Sandra L., ed. *God Is No Stranger.* Grand Rapids, Mich.: Baptist Haiti Mission, 1970. An English translation of profoundly simple prayers of Haitian Christians recently converted from native religions, adaptable for liturgical use as invitations to worship, intercessions, confessions, and thanksgivings. Order from: Baptist Haiti Mission, 1537 Plainfield Avenue, NE, Grand Rapids, MI 49505.

Carden, John, ed. *With All God's People: The New Ecumenical Prayer Cycle.* 2 vols. Geneva: World Council of Churches, 1989. Volume 1 is a rich treasury of prayers from nationalities around the globe, arranged in a weekly cycle covering one year. Volume 2 contains full liturgies, including songs in native languages that follow the liturgical year.

de Gruchy, John W., ed. *Cry Justice: Prayers, Meditations, and Readings from South Africa.* Maryknoll, N.Y.: Orbis Books, 1986. A unique volume of worship materials from native Christians in South Africa, including passionate prayers, litanies, readings, and songs (with music) in the interest of freedom and justice.

The Feast of Life. New York: World Council of Churches, 1983. The eucharistic liturgy used at the Vancouver Assembly, incorporating the doctrinal convergences expressed in the "Baptism, Eucharist and Ministry" document. In four languages.

Gittins, Anthony. *Heart of Prayer: African, Jewish and Biblical Prayers.* London: Collins Liturgical Publications, 1985. A superb resource containing 150 African prayers from fifty African societies as well as prayers from Jewish worship. The prayers are arranged thematically and are well-indexed.

González, Justo and Catherine. *In Accord: Let Us Worship.* New York: Friendship Press, 1981. Excellent resources for multiracial, multicultural worship, although limited in number. A helpful discussion of the nature and purpose of multicultural worship.

Hope, Anne. *Torch in the Night: Worship Resources from South Africa.* New York: Friendship Press, 1989. Ritual, stories, poems, and responsive readings built around twelve worship themes.

Hymns from the Four Winds: A Collection of Asian American Hymns. Nashville: Abingdon Press, 1983. An impressive collection of hymns sung in Asian American congregations.

In Spirit and in Truth: A Worship Book. Geneva: World Council of Churches, 1991. The worship resources for the Seventh Assembly of the World Council of Churches in Canberra, containing multicultural responsive readings, prayers, creeds and affirmations, and hymns (with music) in various languages. A rich and valuable ecumenical resource. Order from: WCC Distribution Center, Box 346, Route 222 and Sharadin Road, Kutztown, PA 19530.

Jesus Christ—the Life of the World. Geneva: World Council of Churches, 1983. The worship materials used in the Sixth Assembly of the World Council of Churches in Vancouver. For description and ordering address, see above, *In Spirit and in Truth*.

Link, Hans-Georg, ed. *Confessing Our Faith Around the World*. 4 vols. Geneva: World Council of Churches, 1983-85. Ecumenical papers of the Faith and Order Commission of the World Council of Churches from throughout the world, containing a considerable number of worship materials: prayers, confessionals, creeds, and eucharistic liturgies.

Loh, I-to, ed. *African Songs of Worship*. Geneva: World Council of Churches, 1986. Twenty-one songs from various African countries (with music), some with English translations. Includes an audiocasette of excerpts from live performances.

Mbiti, John S. *The Prayers of African Religion*. Maryknoll, N.Y.: Orbis Books, 1975. Stimulating African prayers for a variety of occasions, with explanation and commentary by the author.

Ortmayer, Roger, ed. *Sing and Pray and Shout Hurray!* New York: Friendship Press, 1974. Despite its rather flip title, this book contains serious and usable liturgical materials, including a few full liturgies (and nine songs), from Christian communities around the globe.

Pawelzik, Fritz, ed. *I Lie on My Mat and Pray: Prayers of Young Africans*. New York: Friendship Press, 1964. Passionate prayers, both personal and social, from young African Christians. While they are not written as liturgical prayers, most of them could be adapted for public worship.

————. *I Sing Your Praise All the Day Long: Young Africans at Prayer*. New York: Friendship Press, 1967. See above.

Runcie, Robert, and Basil Hume. *Prayers for Peace*. London: SPCK, 1987. New and old prayers for peace from various international religions.

Schellman, James. *Consultation on Common Texts: Ecumenical Services of Prayer*. Mahwah, N.Y.: Paulist Press, 1983. Prayer services containing readings, psalms, and hymns for ecumenical worship.

Sharpe, J. Ed. *American Indian Prayers and Poetry*. Cherokee, N.C.: Cherokee Publications, 1985. Order from: Box 256, Cherokee, NC 28719.
A booklet of prayers, poems, and sayings from various tribes of Native Americans. It includes a Native American version of the Lord's Prayer and the Twenty-Third Psalm.

Shorter, Aylward. *Prayer in the Religious Traditions of Africa*. New York: Oxford University Press, 1975. Stunning prayers from native Africans. Because they hold so closely to native styles and concepts, the prayers will often have to be modified for use in liturgies elsewhere, but they have much to offer for enriching traditional prayer language.

Thurian, Max, and Geoffrey Wainwright, eds. *Baptism and Eucharist: Ecumenical Convergence in Celebration*. Grand Rapids, Mich.: Wm. B. Eerdmans, 1983. Prayers and full baptismal and eucharistic liturgies from Christian congregations around the world. A baptismal and eucharistic liturgy based on the Lima Document is included, composed by the authors.

Union Prayer Book for Jewish Worship. rev. ed. New York: Central Conference of American Rabbis, 1977. Volume I, revised, is the popular prayerbook of contemporary Jewish worship, containing complete worship liturgies and an abundance of rich prayers, beautifully worded.

Vamos Caminando: A Peruvian Catechism. Maryknoll, N.Y.: Orbis Books, 1985. A study book from Peru with comments, readings, poems, and stories of Christians in a Two-Thirds World country; easily adaptable for liturgical use.

Worship Planning Guide. Memphis: Baptist Peace Fellowship, 1990. Worship suggestions and resources that address racism and poverty in our churches and society, based on the work of Dr. Martin Luther King, Jr. Order from: 499 Patterson St., Memphis, TN 38111.

Contemporary Prayers

Anderson, Vienna Cobb. *Prayers of Our Hearts in Word and Action.* (New York: Crossroad, 1991). An extraordinary collection of prayers composed by the author for use in her parish. The prayers address a number of difficult contemporary conditions, always with sensitivity and appropriate language.

Appleton, George, ed. *The Oxford Book of Prayer.* New York: Oxford University Press, 1985. Few prayers with a contemporary ring can be found in this anthology, but a significant number of prayers from Two-Thirds Nations are included.

Baille, John. *A Diary of Private Prayer.* New York: Charles Scribner's Sons, 1978. rev. ed. Somehow this classic book still speaks in the modern idiom! Though the prayers are personal in nature, they are adaptable for public worship.

Campbell, Ernest T. *Where Cross the Crowded Ways.* New York: New York Associated Press, 1973. Unfortunately out of print, the book contains prayers arising directly out human life experience, worded by one of the best practitioners of the art.

Daily Prayer: The Worship of God. Philadelphia: Westminster Press, 1987. Simple, traditional orders for daily prayer. The prayers are rather general and contemplative in nature, yet the language is contemporary.

Falla, Terry C. *Be Our Freedom, Lord: Responsive Prayers and Readings for Contemporary Worship.* Grand Rapids, Mich.: Wm. B. Eerdmans, 1981. Although these prayers are rather dated now, this is still a usable resource for prayers that reflect life in the world around us.

Fike, Earle W., Jr. *Please Pray with Me: Prayers for People at Worship.* Elgin, Ill.: Brethren Press, 1990. A volume of fifty-five prayers used by the author in his parish. The prayers are simple, clear, and fresh, written in everyday language about everyday situations.

Glaser, Chris. *Coming Out to God: Prayers for Lesbians and Gay Men, Their Families and Friends.* Louisville: Westminster/John Knox, 1990. These are personal prayers, but they furnish unique insights into the needs and interests of persons who are lesbian and gay, and so may be useful for informing general corporate prayers.

Griolet, Pierre. *You Call Us Together: Prayers for the Christian Assembly*. Trans. Edmond Bonin. New York: Paulist Press, 1972. Insightful prayers for worship on the conservative side.

Loder, Ted. *Guerrillas of Grace*. San Diego: LuraMedia, 1984. The unusual title comes from the fact that guerrillas try to reclaim a territory. These prayers rumble up against the "principalities and powers" in interesting images. Prayer leaders should have this book: its images are vivid but within liturgical limits.

Moore, Joseph. *Prayers for a New Generation: A Prayerbook for Teens*. Mahwah, N.J.: Paulist Press, 1991. A prayerbook oriented toward life experiences of young people.

Morley, Janet, and Hannah Ward, eds. *Celebrating Women*. Wilton, Conn.: Morehouse-Barlow, 1986. More than fifty prayers, litanies, meditations, and poems by women from many denominations, sponsored by "Movement for the Ordination of Women" (MOW) in Great Britain.

Ohler, Frederick. *Better Than Nice and Other Unconventional Prayers*. Louisville: Westminster/John Knox, 1989. The book is aptly named: the prayers are better than nice, and they are unconventional. They are unpretentious, honest, and clear—prayers prayed by the author in his church. His style is so unique that use of the prayers by others will require rephrasing.

Pearson, Roy. *Prayers for All Occasions: For Pastors and Lay Leaders*. Valley Forge: Judson Press, 1990. Prayers in the traditional mode, unfortunately lacking in explicit contemporary reference.

Phifer, Kenneth G. *A Book of Uncommon Prayer*. Nashville: Upper Room Press, 1983. Although written in the first-person singular and intended for private devotional use, these insightful prayers of contemporary life-experiences can be made suitable for the public assembly.

Phillips, E. Lee. *Prayers for Our Day*. Atlanta: John Knox Press, 1982. Although the author uses Tudor English with reference to God, the prayers are well-written and often contain lists of everyday experiences that may suggest petitions for contemporary public prayers.

Prayers for Worship. Liturgical Publications Inc., 2875 South James Drive, New Berlin, WI 53151 (800) 876-4574. A subscription service that provides prayers for Sunday liturgies. Ecumenical in scope, it follows the liturgical year.

Quoist, Michel. *New Prayers*. New York: Crossroad/Continuum, 1990. The French priest's prayers and meditations are sometimes painful and troubling but are born out of the heart of human experience. See also the author's *Prayers* (Kansas City: Sheed and Ward, 1963).

Roberts, Elizabeth, and Elias Amidan. *Earth Prayers from Around the World*. San Francisco: Harper San Francisco, 1991. This book contains 365 prayers, poems, and invocations in behalf of the earth and its resources.

Rowthorn, Jeffery W. *The Wideness of God's Mercy: Litanies to Enlarge Our Prayer*. 2 vols. Minneapolis: Seabury Press, 1985. The second volume

("Prayers for the World"), especially, is a solid repertory of contemporary, multicultural prayers, often written in bold and imaginative strokes. An excellent resource.

Sawyer, Beverly. *Singer of Seasons: The Prayers of Beverly Sawyer.* Little Rock: August House, 1982. Prayers prayed by the author in the worship services of the church she serves. The prayers come right out of daily human experience and are composed with sensitivity and insight—and with a pastor's heart.

Schaffran, Janet, and Pat Kozak. *More Than Words: Prayer and Ritual for Inclusive Communities.* Oak Park, Ill.: Meyer-Stone Books, 1988. The book contains a number of liturgies, readings, and prayers centering, for the most part, on feminist and justice issues worded in imaginative and artistic ways.

Thorne, Leo S., ed. *Prayers from Riverside.* New York: Pilgrim Press, 1983. A mixed bag of prayers prayed at Riverside Church in New York City through the years. Some will be suggestive and helpful, others not. The prayers are arranged to follow the liturgical year.

Wade, David L. *Lord Forgive Me: Prayers of Confession.* Lima, Oh.: C.S.S. Publishing Company, Cycle B: 1987, Cycle C: 1988, Cycle A: 1989. Prayers composed for the author's campus ministries. They are wide-ranging, honest, and in colloquial language—probably too informal for traditional worship liturgies.

Winter, Miriam Therese. *WomanPrayer WomanSong: Resources for Ritual.* Oak Park, Ill.: Meyer-Stone Books, 1987. Liturgies and songs mostly comprise this volume, but there are several prayers as well that use feminist imagery effectively.

[Note: This list does not include the growing number of prayer resource publications that are keyed to the lectionary. Such a comprehensive use of the lectionary in liturgy, though, is questionable in that 1) the biblical texts may be reduced either to thematic or "catch-all" interpretations, and 2) the integrity of each component of the liturgy may be compromised.] Examples:

Bayler, Lavon. *Fresh Winds of the Spirit: Liturgical Resources for Year A, Whispers of God: Liturgical Resources for Year B,* and *Refreshing Rains of the Living Word: Liturgical Resources for Year C.* New York: Pilgrim Press, 1986, 1987, 1988.

Hostetter, David B. *Psalms and Prayers for Congregational Participation.* Lima, Oh.: C.S.S. Publishing Co., 1983–85. Years A, B, C.

Kirk, James G. *When We Gather: A Book of Prayers for Worship.* Philadelphia: Geneva Press, 1983. Years A, B, C.

Mazziotta, Richard. *We Pray to the Lord: General Intercessions Based on the Scriptural Readings for Sundays and Holy Days.* Notre Dame: Ave Maria Press, 1984.

Ramshaw, Gail, ed. *Intercessions for the Christian People, Cycles A, B, C.* New York: Pueblo Publishing, 1988.

Tilson, Everett, and Phyllis Cole. *Litanies and Other Prayers for the Common Lectionary.* Nashville: Abingdon Press, 1989. Years A, B.

Composing and Leading Corporate Prayers

Buttrick, David G. "On Liturgical Language." *Reformed Liturgy and Music* 15 (Winter 1981), 74–82. An invaluable resource on using "public language" in liturgical speech in an extraordinary way. The author discusses style, form, depiction, and cadence of liturgical language, especially with reference to contemporary corporate prayer.

Fendall, Lon. "How to Pray For (and Against) Leaders in Government." *Christianity Today* 27 (17 June 1983), 14–16. An interesting discussion of corporate prayers with reference to public leaders, based on Psalm 72 and 1 Samuel 15, in which the major concerns are justice, peace and stability, true prosperity, and ultimate patriotism.

Finn, Peter C., and James M. Schellman, eds. *Shaping English Liturgy: Studies in Honor of Archbishop Denis Hurley.* Washington, D.C.: Pastoral Press, 1990. See especially pp. 242-55 in "Original Texts: Beginnings, Present Projects, Guidelines," by H. Kathleen Hughes, for a helpful commentary on the guidelines for composing liturgical prayers drawn up by the ICEL (see chap. 3). The article offers concise explanations, suggestions, and examples for each of the twenty-four guidelines. An invaluable aid.

Fitzgerald, Timothy. "General Intercessions." *Liturgy 90* 21 (May/June 1990 and July 1990), 9–12, 4–15. Two articles from a Catholic perspective that analyze the purpose of liturgical intercessory prayer, provide helpful suggestions for wording the intercessions, and evaluate three collections of contemporary prayers.

Hall, Stuart G. "The Prayer of the Church: What We Ask and How We Ask It." *The Expository Times* 96 (December 1984), 73–77. The section "The content of prayers" is especially helpful, although the author draws an extremely narrow interpretation of what is didactic and subjective in public prayers.

Hedrick, William K. "Prayer in Worship." *Austin Seminary Bulletin: Faculty Edition* 101 (October 1985), 45–50. A general discussion of the values and dangers of spontaneous prayers, prayers written by others, and self-prepared prayers in worship.

Henderson, J. Frank, Kathleen Quinn, and Stephen Larson. "General Intercessions." *Liturgy, Justice and the Reign of God.* New York: Paulist Press, 1989, 71. A brief but wide-ranging list of suggestions for wording intercessions, especially for peace and justice.

Hoffman, Lawrence A. *The Art of Public Prayer: Not for Clergy Only.* Washington, D.C.: Pastoral Press, 1989. A significant study on the language, not only of public prayer, but of the liturgy as a whole, containing only limited instruction on *how* to compose artful public prayers.

Holt, Bradley P. "Common Prayer and Local/Global Mission." *Word and World: Theology for Christian Ministry* 5 (Spring 1985), 199–205. An extremely helpful discussion of the theological factors that support public prayers of global scope concerned with peace and justice. Practical suggestions for framing such prayers are included.

Hovda, Robert. "The Amen Corner." *Worship* 60 (November 1986). An important essay on the language and formulaic model of general intercessions, prompting responses from John A. Melloh and Joyce Zimmerman (see below) that expand the discussion substantially.

————. *Dry Bones: Living Worship Guides to Good Liturgy.* Washington, D.C.: Liturgical Conference, 1973. The chapter "Praying Commonly" is especially helpful in this book about lively liturgical language.

Hughes, Kathleen. *Lay Presiding: The Art of Leading Prayer.* Washington, D.C.: Pastoral Press, 1988. The book primarily treats questions concerning Catholic lay leadership, but includes general suggestions for wording prayers along with guidelines published by the International Commission on English in the Liturgy.

Hurd, Bob. "The Prayer of the Faithful: Finding the Assembly's Voice." *Liturgy* 8 (Spring 1990), 52–59. A discussion of spontaneous congregational participation in intercessory prayers, with an interesting plan for incorporating the petitions into a congregational hymn.

Huxhold, Harry N. "What Is the Place of Pastoral Prayer in the Context of Worship?" *Encounter: Creative Theological Scholarship* 43 (Autumn 1982), 395–400. A study of the tension between spontaneous and formal liturgical prayer, providing principles for wording prayers that reflect personal, current, parochial, and general concerns.

Melloh, John A. "The General Intercessions Revisited." *Worship* 61 (March 1987), 152–62. A scholarly response to Robert Hovda's essay (see above) on the congregational context of prayer intercessions and the use of oral language appropriate to that context. The author calls upon various literary scholars for support.

Patrick, Dale, and James Kratz. "Making the Pastoral Prayer an Act of the Congregation." *Encounter: Creative Theological Scholarship* 51 (Spring 1990), 183–89. A discussion of bidding prayers in the free church tradition.

Perdue, Harold C. "Developing the Pastoral Prayer." *The Christian Ministry* 20 (May/June 1989), 24–25. A brief article on composing corporate prayers based on hymns.

Scagnelli, Peter. "The General Intercessions." *Sourcebook for Sundays and Seasons.* Chicago: Liturgy Training Publications, 1988. Pages 50–52 offer detailed suggestions for structuring prayer intercessions for Catholic worship.

Steen, Norman. "Let Us Pray: Turning a Monologue into the Prayers of the People." *Reformed Worship* 11 (Spring 1989), 30–34. A general discussion of "bidding" and other prayer forms that help involve the congregation.

Stevick, Daniel B. *Language in Worship: Reflections on a Crisis.* New York: Seabury Press, 1970. Although dated now, this is a comprehensive discussion on modernizing the language of liturgy. No lists of instructions or guidelines are provided, but the book as a whole is useful for designing corporate prayers.

Vander Beek, William. "Priestly Prayers: Intercessions for the Church and World." *Reformed Worship* 11 (Spring 1989), 30–34. A brief but helpful discussion on using concrete and specific prayer language, offering practical suggestions and guidelines.

Weil, Louis. *Gathered to Pray: Understanding Liturgical Prayer*. Cambridge, Mass.: Cowley Publications, 1986. An Anglican discussion of liturgical prayer, including a defense of the linguistic revisions of the 1979 *Book of Common Prayer*.

Willimon, William H. *Preaching and Leading Worship*. Philadelphia: Westminster Press, 1984. Chapter 3, on "Public Prayer," includes five guidelines for composing free prayers and four guidelines for the use of language in free prayers.

Zimmerman, Joyce A. "The General Intercessions: Yet Another Visit." *Worship* 65 (July 1991), 306–19. A response to essays by Robert Hovda and, subsequently, John Melloh (see above) in which the work of language theorists is used to make practical suggestions for creating formulas and wording for prayer petitions and intercessions.

Hymnbooks

(See also listings under "Ecumenical Liturgical Resources")

Anderson, Fred R. *Singing Psalms of Joy and Praise*. Philadelphia: Westminster Press, 1986. Fifty-two of the biblical psalms written in contemporary verse to be sung to familiar hymn tunes.

Berthier, Jacques. *Music from Taizé*. 2 vols. Chicago: G.I.A. Publications, Inc., 1978, 1982. Responses, litanies, acclamations, and canons from the famous Taizé community near Cluny, France, written in simple, singable styles by Father Berthier.

Braun, H. Myron. *Companion to the Book of Hymns Supplement*. Nashville: United Methodist Church, 1982.

Cantate Domino: An Ecumenical Hymn Book. New York: World Council of Churches, 1980. An excellent resource of two hundred hymns from throughout the world in various languages but with English translations.

The Collegeville Hymnal. Collegeville, Minn.: Liturgical Press, 1990. Includes 480 hymns, old and new, in addition to Catholic mass and service music. A Catholic hymnal, but ecumenical in scope with much diversity and a variety of liturgical options. Some concern for inclusive language.

Doran, Carol, and Thomas H. Troeger. *New Hymns for the Lectionary: To Glorify the Maker's Name*. New York: Oxford University Press, 1986. Includes fifty-two hymns with original tunes (but in meters that can be put to traditional tunes) based on biblical texts, written in fresh, clear contemporary language and a uniformly artistic style. Inclusive language throughout.

Duck, Ruth C., and Michael G. Bausch, eds. *Everflowing Streams: Songs for Worship*. New York: Pilgrim Press, 1981. Includes eighty-seven hymns and songs, many of them new and in the folk style. The language of traditional hymns in the volume has been altered to be gender-inclusive.

————. *Flames of the Spirit*. New York: Pilgrim Press, 1981. The same as above, except that more of the hymns reflect a concern for justice issues, and hymns for special occasions have been added.

Eslinger, Elise E., ed. *The Upper Room Worshipbook*. Nashville: Upper Room, 1985. An interesting variety of usable, singable church music: general hymns, folk songs, canticles, responses and rounds, psalmody, and service music in multiple styles: traditional, ethnic, and contemporary. Inclusive language.

Huber, Jane Parker. *A Singing Faith*. Philadelphia: Westminster Press, 1987. Includes seventy-three well-written hymns, most of which are set to familiar tunes, that cover a broad spectrum of subjects. A brief commentary is provided for each. Some of these hymns appear in recently published denominational hymnals, and the author gives permission to reprint the words in church worship bulletins. (Would that other collections did the same!)

The Hymnal 1982. New York: Church Hymnal Corporation, 1985. The revised hymnal of the Episcopal Church, solidly in the classical tradition, but including a number of hymns written by contemporary hymnwriters. Little attention is given to gender-inclusive language.

Hymns from the Four Winds: A Collection of Asian American Hymns. Nashville: Abingdon Press, 1983. A noteworthy repertory of 125 hymns in Asian musical styles. Explanatory notes and performance suggestions are included. Two-thirds of the texts are newly written, and many of the tunes are simple enough to be sung by congregations in the United States. General inclusive language.

The Iona Community Worship Book. Iona, Scotland: Wild Goose Publications, 1988. A book of songs, prayers, and liturgies from the famed Iona Community in Scotland, written by members of the community. Order from: St. Mutual Books, 521 5th Avenue, New York, NY 10175.

Jabusch, Willard F. *The Lord Is Here*. Chicago: Musica Pacis,1989. The latest of twelve music books by the author. Twenty-five songs and hymns in generally traditional and gender-specific language. The author permits reproduction of his work in church worship bulletins.

Jesus Christ—the Life of the World: Hymns. New York: World Council of Churches, 1983. A valuable collection of hymns in four languages used in the liturgy at the Vancouver Assembly of the World Council of Churches.

Kaan, Fred, and Doreen Potter. *Break Not the Circle: Twenty New Hymns*. Carol Stream, Ill.: Agape, 1975. Kaan's hymns are among the best being written today: Erik Routley, in this collection, gives him a glowing review. Hymnwriter and composer combine to make singing new hymns delightful, exciting and, especially, enjoyable.

Lead Me, Guide Me: The African American Catholic Hymnal. Chicago: G.I.A. Publications, Inc., 1987. A complete hymnal containing 561 hymns, songs, and service music: an interesting combination of traditional hymns, spirituals, and folk songs used primarily in African American Catholic Church liturgies.

Lodge, Ann, ed. *Creation Sings*. Philadelphia: Geneva Press, 1979. A booklet of new songs in inclusive language and imagery.

Loh, I-to, ed. *African Songs of Worship*. New York: World Council of Churches, 1987. A booklet of African songs with music.

Lutheran Book of Worship. Minneapolis: Augsburg, 1978. A grand volume containing the complete Lutheran liturgies (words and music), the Psalter, lectionary, and 569 canticles, hymns, and songs. The hymnody, however, for the most part, is traditional and the language in reference to God is androcentric.

NewSong. Hope Publishing Company, Carol Stream, IL 60188. Published three times a year, the periodical is edited by Brian Wren, the internationally acclaimed hymnwriter. Each issue contains articles on hymnody and features four new hymns of high quality.

The Presbyterian Hymnal: Hymns, Psalms, and Spiritual Songs. Louisville: Westminster/John Knox, 1990. A noteworthy collection of six hundred hymns, songs, and psalms drawn from a variety of musical styles. Included are hymns from other countries, some in native languages, and an impressive assortment of hymns by contemporary hymnwriters. Inclusive language is used where not prohibitive.

Psalter Hymnal. Grand Rapids, Mich.: Christian Reformed Church, 1987. An outstanding church hymnal in the Reformed tradition, containing a complete metrical psalter, biblical songs, 405 hymns and responses, and the denomination's creedal, doctrinal, and liturgical forms and resources. Twentieth-century hymnody and ethnic texts and tunes are included. Inclusive language with reference to humans.

Resource Collection of Hymns and Service Music for the Liturgy. Chicago: G.I.A. Publications, Inc., 1981. In addition to 247 traditional hymns, this volume contains 105 new hymns, canticles, and service music, but generally in traditional and gender-specific language. The publishers give permission to reproduce hymns in worship bulletins.

Routley, Erik, ed. *Rejoice in the Lord: A Hymn Companion to the Scriptures*. Grand Rapids, Mich.: Wm. B. Eerdmans, 1985. A classic collection of the best hymns of the church, most of them old but some written by contemporary authors, including nine by Routley himself. Gender-neutral language with reference to humans.

Schaap, David P., and John Worst, eds. *Songs of Rejoicing*. New Brunswick, N.J.: Selah Publishing Company, 1989. An excellent collection of 254 new hymns—words, music, harmonizations—by both well known and new contemporary church musicians, in styles ranging from traditional to folk. A superb supplement to traditional hymnals. Order from Box 103, Accord, NY 12404.

Sing to God: Songs and Hymns for Christian Education. New York: United Church Press, 1984. An eminently useful collection of musical materials suitable for use by children and adults.

Songs of Zion. Nashville: Abingdon Press, 1981. A valuable collection of songs of the African American worship experience, including less familiar spirituals and contemporary service music by William Farley Smith and others. There are several brief but fascinating pages that explain and describe the music of African American worship.

Songs of Hope and Peace. New York: Pilgrim Press, 1988. Fifty-two new songs with mostly new but singable tunes. Written by members of the United Church of Christ, they enlarge on the themes of unity, justice, and hope.

Ten New Hymns on Aging and the Later Years. American Association of Retired Persons: 1909 K St., NW, Washington, DC 20049. Ten hymns of mixed quality that center on growing old, sung to traditional tunes. The booklet is free of charge and is available from AARP.

The United Methodist Hymnal. Nashville: United Methodist Publishing House, 1989. Although it has kept a large inventory of the more individualistic gospel songs, this is an outstanding collection of many types of good hymnody from around the world, much of it by contemporary hymnwriters. It includes a Psalter and worship liturgies, and has altered some language to be sex- and race-inclusive.

Young, Carlton R., ed. *Supplement to the Book of Hymns.* Nashville: United Methodist Publishing House, 1982. An interesting mixture of 127 songs and hymns, many representing ethnic minorities and including "standard" and "pop" songs (some now included in the new United Methodist hymnal), in gender-inclusive language.

Worship. 3d ed. Chicago: G.I.A. Publications, 1986. Along with its companion volume, *Gather,* a solid repertory of hymns of quality, traditional and contemporary, in several genres. Contains Catholic service music, a full lectionary, and liturgical prayers.

The Worshiping Church: A Hymnal. Carol Stream, Ill.: Hope Publishing Company, 1990. Quite an eclectic collection of hymnody, including about 240 hymns and songs by contemporary writers. A superfluous number are "praise songs," that is, simple, repetitive choruses, some might say jingles. The volume includes psalms and canticles and almost every standard gospel song in the repertory of evangelical worship. Some sexist human-language in hymns has been made gender-neutral.

Worst, John, and David Schaap, eds. *Songs of Rejoicing: Hymns for Worship, Meditation and Praise.* New Brunswick, N.J.: Selah Publishing Company, 1989. A comprehensive collection of high-quality new hymns, many by established contemporary hymnwriters. A noteworthy hymnal supplement.

Wren, Brian. *Faith Looking Forward.* Carol Stream, Ill.: Hope Publishing Co., 1983. Forty-nine hymns of the highest quality by arguably the best living hymnwriter today. The hymns are unquestionably ecumenical, inclusive, stimulating, and profoundly theological. Many of these hymns can be found in the new denominational hymnals as well.

————. *Praising a Mystery.* Carol Stream, Ill.: Hope Publishing Co., 1986. See above.

Religious News Periodicals

America. Jesuit Order of the Catholic Church. A progressive journal that interprets and evaluates current events from both a Catholic and catholic perspective: Box 77274, Atlanta, GA 30357.

The Christian Century. Independently published. An ecumenical progressive journal of commentary on the contemporary social scene: 5615 West Cermak, Cicero, IL 60650.

Christianity and Crisis: A Christian Journal of Opinion. An independent journal founded by Reinhold Niebuhr. Today some of the most respected authorities on Christian social issues serve on its board and staff: 537 West 121 St., New York, NY 10027.

Christianity Today. Independently published. A conservative/evangelical commentary on the contemporary social scene: Box 11618, Des Moines, IA 50340.

Christian Social Action. Board of Church and Society, United Methodist Church. The social issues periodical of the United Methodist Church: 100 Maryland Avenue, NW, Washington, DC 20002.

Church and Society. Presbyterian Church (U.S.A.). The social issues periodical of the Presbyterian Church (U.S.A.): 100 Witherspoon Street, Louisville, KY 40202.

Church and State. Americans United for Separation of Church and State. A serious ecumenical journal concerned with church-state justice issues: 8120 Fenton Street, Silver Spring, MD 20910.

CALC Report. Clergy and Laity Concerned. An ecumenical, multinational, multicultural journal for persons of conscience from all walks of life: 340 Mead Road, Decatur, GA 30030.

Current Thoughts & Trends. The Navigators. A summary of news and commentary from more than forty major Christian publications and secular magazines with the local pastor in view: P.O. Box 35004, Colorado Springs, CO 80935.

Ecumenical Press Service. The World Council of Churches. In newsletter format, coverage of church/society activities worldwide: Box 2100, CH-1211, Geneva 2 Switzerland.

Fellowship. The Fellowship of Reconciliation. An ecumenical journal concerned primarily with peace and justice issues worldwide: 523 North Broadway, Nyack, NY 10960.

Friends Journal. Friends Publishing Corporation. The social issues periodical of the Society of Friends: 1501 Cherry Street, Philadelphia, PA 19102.

Interfaith Impact for Justice and Peace. Independent, nondenominational. A progressive political advocacy publication, connecting Washington, D.C., with the local congregation: 110 Maryland Avenue NE, Washington, DC 20002.

National Catholic Reporter. National Catholic Reporter Publishing Company. One of several Catholic journals on social issues; this one is the most independent: Box 419281, Kansas City, MO 64141.

NEWS/VIEWS. Atlanta Friends Meeting. A collection of articles gathered from a broad spectrum of newspapers and periodicals on the environment, peace and justice, and human rights: 1700 W. Paces Ferry Road, NW, Atlanta, GA 38327.

The Other Side. Jubilee, Inc. An independent Christian progressive journal of advocacy and commentary on social issues; magazine format, with a lively style and straightforward approach: 300 West Apsley Street, Philadelphia, PA 19144.

Sojourners. Sojourners, Inc. The magazine of Christian social conscience published by an evangelical Christian community in Washington, D.C.: Box 29972, Washington, DC 20017.

United Church News. United Church of Christ. The social issues paper of the United Church of Christ: 105 Madison Avenue, New York, NY 10016.

The Witness. Episcopal Church Publishing Company. The social issues periodical of the Episcopal Church: 1249 Washington Boulevard, Suite 3115, Detroit, MI 48226-1868.

World Vision. The publication of the Christian humanitarian agency emphasizing issues of poverty, hunger, and the environment, but generally avoiding politically controversial issues: 919 West Huntington Drive, Monrovia, CA 91016.

INDEX

INDEX

Messerli, Carlos H., 45 n.35, 46 n.37
Micklem, Caryl, 90
Mieir, Audrey, 91
Miffleton, Jack, 125 n.72
Miller, Donald, 117 n.57
Mills, C. Wright, 43 n.27
Mills, Pauline, 91
Minear, Paul S., 4 n.2
Mitchell, Leonel L., 135 n.7
Mol, Laura, 98 n.9
Morley, Janet, 71 n.34
Mowinckel, Sigmund, 34
Muehl, William, 65, 67

Native Americans, 95, 109, 110 n.34, 139, 152, 156-57
Neale, John Mason, 84
Newsome, Carol A., 105 n.26
Niebuhr, H. Richard, 26-27

Ortmayer, Roger, 144 n.30, 150 n.40

Palmer, Parker J., 68
Patterson, James, 117 n.55
Patterson, Joy, 88-9
Paul, apostle, 4-7, 21, 28, 130
Peter, apostle, 6 n.10, 21, 22, 38
Polman, Bert, 91 n.77
Post, Marie J., 86-87
Postman, Niel, 15 n.33
Prayer, liturgical
  composing of, 80-83
  congregationally inclusive, 122-28
  contextual, 74-80
  for enemies, 120, 132-33
  for outcasts, 131-32
  global in scope, 129-33
  of confession, 9, 45, 60-62
  of intercession, 11-12, 56-59, 68-72, 74-78, 124, 127
  of thanksgiving, 10, 58-59, 72, 124, 125, 126-27, 141-43
  postures, 112
  requests, audible, 58
  trinitarian concerns of, 83
Preaching, 10-11
  and liturgy, 22
  as contextual, 72-74
  language of, 50-52
  biblical understanding of, 19-21
  teaching, 41

Quinn, Kathleen, 29 n.67

Radner, Ephraim, 16 n.36
Ramshaw, Gail, 35 n.7, 36, 41, 48 n.45, 98 n.9, 100 n.11, 103
Rayan, Samuel, 141
Reagan, Ronald, 132
Religious periodicals, use of, 74
Richard, Pablo, 141 n.22
Ringe, Sharon H., 105 n.26
Robb, Tom, 32 n.3
Rogers, Isabel Wood, 98 n.7
Roman, Alfonso, 110
Romero, Oscar, 30, 78
Routley, Erik, 84, 86, 86 n.59, 90
Rowan, William P., 86 n.59
Rowthorn, Jeffery, 85
Roy, Louis, 102 n.20
Rukeyser, Louis, 43
Runyon, Theodore, 9 n.19
Russell, Letty, 105 n.26

Sacraments, the, 4, 5, 24-25
Saliers, Don, 36
Sandburg, Carl, 94, 95
Schellman, James M., 81 n.47
Scripture, liturgical response to, 143, 154
Seerveld, Calvin, 87
Shelby Baptist Association, 14 n.29
Shepherd, Thomas B., 115 n.50
Shorney, George H., 17 n.38
Shorter, Aylward, 142 n.25
Simmons, Morgan, 86 n.62
Smith, Henry, 91
Smith, Leonard, 91
Smith, Michael, W., 91
Smith, William Farley, 87 n.68
Smith, William S., 116 n.53
Spirit, Holy, 6, 20-21, 22, 25, 28, 64, 79, 81, 83, 93, 139, 157
Stein, Jock, 92 n.78
Stigall, Robert, 86 n.59
Stone, Chuck, 95, n.2

Tamez, Elsa, 138
Thompson, William D., 52
Throckmorton, Burton H., 48 n.43
Thurian, Max, 143 n.28
Tilton, Robert, 14 n.28

Tirabassi, Maren C., 105 nn.25, 26
Toles, Shelanda, 1
Toporoski, Richard, 78 n.42
Torres, Sergio, 141 n.23
Troeger, Thomas H., 56, 84, 85 n.56, 86, 86 n.61, 90, 93
Tubman, Harriet, 30
Tucker, F. Bland, 85

Vajta, Vilmos, 71 n.35
Van Seeters, Arthur, 74 n.38
Vanderhaar, Gerard A., 119
Vatican II, 9, 16, 16 n.37, 35, 37, 134 n.6
Vos, Wiebe, 71 n.35

Wainwright, Geoffrey, 17, 25, 28-29, 143 n.28
Ward, Hanna, 71 n.34
Watts, Isaac, 83-84, 85
Webber, Christopher, 84, 86
Webber, Robert, 91 n.76
Wesley, John, 84, 130
Wesley Theological Seminary, 18
Westendorf, Omer, 119 n.63
White, James F., 57, 80
Wilder, Amos, 31, 38, 50
Williams, Joseph M., 43 n.27
Williamson, Clark, 39 n.19, 41 n.24
Wink, Walter, 69
Winter, Miriam Therese, 105 n.26
World Council of Churches, the, 17, 114
Worship
  See Liturgy
Worshipbooks, liturgical
  Episcopal, 25, 134 n.6
  Lutheran, 24, 45, 68, 101
  Presbyterian, 29, 45-46, 101
  United Church of Christ, 25, 101, 114 n.48, 145 n.32
  United Methodist, 24, 30, 101, 145, 147
  See also Prayerbooks
Worship resources, global, 137-58
Wren, Brian, 11, 84, 84 n.55, 85, 86, 87, 88, 98 nn.6, 9
Wynne, Alton Donald, 76

Youngs, Sharon K., 113 n.42, 119 n.63